The Aroma of Czech Cuisine

The Aroma of Czech Cuisine

Denise Mazal Resnerova

TCU PRESS
Fort Worth, Texas

Library of Congress Cataloging-in-Publication Data

Names: Resnerova, Denise Mazal, author.
Title: The aroma of Czech cuisine : original recipes / Denise Mazal Resnerova.
Description: Fort Worth, Texas : TCU Press, [2024] | Summary: "With my cookbook, The Aroma of Czech Cuisine, I am proud to showcase the national Czech food, or as we call it, "Staročeská kuchyně" (recipes of our grandmothers). Throughout the book, notes and mini stories accompany the recipes, unfolding a myriad of facts about Czech culture, recipe origins, folklore, history, and Czech influence in the United States. As the founder of Little Gretel, a Czech restaurant in Boerne, Texas, I am devoted to my craft and to putting smiles on the faces of anyone who takes a bite out of my delectable Kolaches. Since 2009, I have been serving the Boerne and surrounding communities by integrating my traditional Czech culinary skills into the wonderful Texas culture. All the recipes included in this book have been prepared and served in my restaurant for over a decade. These recipes exhibit the finest of Czech culinary tradition and impart the humility of Czech culture by passing down the ability to take simple ingredients and make miracles"-- Provided by publisher.
Identifiers: LCCN 2024003856 | ISBN 9780875658704 (trade paperback)
Subjects: LCSH: Cooking, Czech. | Food habits--Czech Republic--History. | Cooking--Texas--Boerne. | Czech Americans--Food. | Czech Americans--Social life and customs. | LCGFT: Cookbooks.
Classification: LCC TX723.5.C9 R45 2024 | DDC 641.594371--dc23/eng/20240212
LC record available at https://lccn.loc.gov/2024003856

Food photography by Ben Weber.

TCU PRESS

TCU Box 298300
Fort Worth, Texas 76129
www.tcupress.com

Design by Bill Brammer

Contents

Acknowledgments

To my mother, who metaphorically gave me the green light to open my restaurant when she called me at the age of ninety and said, "Denise, I would like to come to the United States and start a new life!" Wow, I thought, and asked her, "What are you going to be doing here?" She replied, "I will bake kolaches and you will sell them!"

And that's how it started. I had an airline ticket for her to come, all her belongings packed in a thirty-six-foot container on a big ship. But on September 11, 2005, she passed away. Instead of her coming here, I used the airline ticket to go bury her. Four years later, I opened my restaurant Little Gretel in Boerne, Texas.

To my daughter, Veronica. Without her, our restaurant would have never happened. She gave me courage to start a restaurant business.

To my husband, Jimmy, who is continuously helping me with my English.

To my dear friends and colleagues from Prague to whom I owe and give big credit—Honza Michálek, former manager of the Czech Culinary Team; Chef Václav Pštros, former owner of the restaurant U Pštrosa; and Pastry Chef Lukaš Skála, owner of Cukrář Skála cafes in Prague.

To the city where I was born, my Prague. If you could transform yourself into a real person, I would give you a huge hug and say: "Thank you, my Prague, for everything you did for me."

Like I do with my mother, I look up to you at all times with respect. Your friendliness and hospitality to visitors from other countries gave me the eagerness to learn and speak several new languages. In spite of your age, you are the most beautiful and elegant lady that gladly poses in front of cameras like an experienced model. The certainty of your beauty helps my confidence. You gave me the strength and focus for every sport I competed in and for my work as a chef. You nourished me with the best-tasting dishes and pastries and taught me good etiquette. Now your recipes are enjoyed here in Texas by my new family and friends. I live far, far away from you now, but I always like to go back to you for advice when I have to make tough decisions. Prague, you are my mother, my mentor. You are magical!

Introduction

The Czech country has always relied on domestic raw materials from local trades, farming, pork and cattle breeding, and hunting. When there was an abundance of food, people quickly learned how to preserve it for days when harvest was slim. Food was not thrown away but smartly converted into different meals and consumed. Today Czechs are healthy and strong people because they eat lots of fresh foods made daily in their homes using the same traditional cooking techniques Czechs have used for centuries. Recipes vary from family to family; the recipes handed down from one generation to the next include a wide array of flavors. Czechs are gourmands, and their taste buds are very well developed.

Now known officially as the Czech Republic, or Czechia for short, this country in Central Europe has been known historically as Czechoslovakia, Bohemia, Böhmen (German), which was a kingdom in the Holy Roman Empire and subsequently a province in the Habsburg's Austrian Empire, then known as known as the Austrian-Hungarian Empire in 1867–1918. Both Bohemia and Czechia were, and are, used to describe the entire Bohemian Crown Lands, which included Czechia, Moravia, and Silesia. Several recipes in this book come from one of these specific regions, which is indicated in the title. When we call a recipe Bohemian, that is because the recipe is very old and originated when Czechia was called Bohemia.

Today the word *Bohemian* is associated with gypsies and people living an artistic and unconventional lifestyle, though it was only through a misunderstanding of geography in nineteenth-century France that gypsies were referred to as Bohemians. Czech is now more commonly used to name the region. Bohemia seems old fashioned and is not used as often, but technically it is still a correct term.

Bohemia, *Boiohaemum* as it was originally known in Latin, comes from the Germanic *Baia-heim*, meaning "Home of the Boii." The Boii were a Celtic tribe, the first inhabitants of our country that we know by name, and lived in this region during the Iron Age. Living in an enclosed space called *oppidum* (plural *oppida)* with up to thirty thousand people, they were extraordinarily advanced but had no writing system.

Early Czech Cuisine

The type of food they had available was quite colorful, and the ingredients have survived to date. The basis of the diet was cereals, from which they prepared various flat breads, porridge, and fermented bread. Sheep, beef, and pork were often cooked in a cauldron or roasted on a spit over burning charcoal. A very popular vegetable was wild garlic, and they also used carrots, leeks, celery, red beets, and turnips. They loved apples, pears, and nuts. They diversified their meals by fishing. Wild game wasn't eaten too often, but they liked venison and wild boar. They used butter or bacon fat. They already knew how to use curd to make cheeses. The most common drink was light beer. In higher society, mead was drunk, and the elite rejoiced with wine.

The Boii diet of our ancestors included foods we eat today.

Mead, *medovina*, is still very popular in Czechia, eastern Europe, and Russia. Mead is an alcoholic drink of fermented honey and water. Probably the oldest alcoholic beverage and basically the ancestor of all alcoholic beverages, it was especially produced in the northern parts of Europe where conditions were not suitable for growing wine grapes. The first mead probably formed in the cavities of the trees where the bees had their hives. When the honey became diluted with rain, bacteria fermented the mix, and the first mead was formed. Mead has been known for centuries for its healing effects. It can help our health if it is consumed in small amounts.

Czech Cuisine of the Fourteenth Century

In the fourteenth century, Bohemian cuisine became more elaborate. The cuisine from this historical period is often viewed as too poor, not very imaginative to today's chefs, but this is not true. This was the era of "the greatest Bohemian ruler," King Charles IV. The time of Charles IV was a golden age for the whole population. Under his rule and for decades afterward, there were no wars. Without war and with robust trade with other nations, the people of that time began to eat more like the way we eat today. It was an era when everything bloomed.

At this time, porridge was a staple—both sweet porridge with fruits and savory porridge with meat, greased with lard for strength. Our ancestors did not know rice or potatoes at that time. They ate different flat breads with cheese. Cattle were bred then, as today, mainly for milk. In times of abundance, people ate pork, and game was served in rich households. Even fish from the sea made it to the table, because Bohemian borders reached as far as the sea, and fish was eaten especially during Lent. For rich people, a luxury dish was sweet porridge sweetened with fruit or honey. Thanks to the Charles IV and more frequent travel, foreign influences invaded our kitchens. Exotic spices were imported; ginger, nutmeg, cinnamon, and also saffron were used, often instead of salt. Vinegar was a common flavoring. People started to eat root vegetables, though not always in the same ways we do today. For example, carrots, which we mainly use in soups, they used to make carrot marmalade.

In those times food was judged vertically. Birds, which fly in the sky, are closer to God. Because of this they were more valuable than root vegetables, which grow in the soil underground and are closer to the devil.

St. Longin's Rotunda and graveyard from the twelfth century. Photograph by Roman Hruška.

Charles Square

King Charles IV had big plans for Prague. He allegedly planned to make Prague the center of the Holy Roman Empire. He started a new viticulture and built New Town.

Charles Square (Karlovo náměsti), one of the largest squares in the world, was the epic center of his plan. Salted fish were sold in the northern part of the square. The southern part traded wood and charcoal. The center of the square was designated for people selling grain.

Then in the fifteenth century, vendors with grain had to move to make space for traders with cattle. The streets called Ječná a Žitná (Barley and Rye) show how the trade center was laid out. Throughout the years, Charles Square became the hub of the cattle trade. When I look back at the location where I grew up, my head starts to spin. I was right in the middle of all the trades.

In the middle of this plaza, Charles IV built a tower dedicated to the holiest body of Jesus Christ, St. Mary, and martyrs St. Felix and St. Adauctus. Charles IV collected holy relics, including fabric from the tablecloth at the Last Supper, the spear of Longinus, thorns from Christ's crown, nails and mildew from Christ's cross, and fabric from Christ's robe.

Once a year since 1354, on Easter Friday, Charles IV let the holy relics be shown. Travelers from all over the world would come to see them. Thousands of people would fill the plaza. Those who died in Prague on this holiday were buried at the cemetery of the St. Longinus rotunda located on street called Na Rybníčku (On the Pond).

Six hundred years later, I lived on Na Rybníčku.
I was in the first grade summer school day care in 1964. Our teachers came up with the idea that we would start our own vegetable garden. It was so exciting. Living in Prague, a big metropolitan city, and right here on my street we could start to grow vegetables!

We all got spades and shovels and started to dig. The soil was pretty soft, and it had lots of small rocks. We were pulling the rocks out and piling them up high until the moment when one of the teachers recognized that these rocks were not rocks but pieces of bone. They immediately stopped us, and our gardening was over.

The buried bones at this cemetery were the bones of the travelers who came from all over the world to see holy relics but did not make it back home and died in the Prague. This first grade school is closed now, and there is a park there. I did not find the whole story about this cemetery until 2020!

The Communist Era

Under Communism, Czech food did not lose its flavor, but it was no longer attractive looking. Food was prepared across the country by *Norms*, the communist recipe book. No one could be creative. Everyone had to go by the rules. The color of food faded, and portions were just slapped on the plate. It had to look the same way in every city and in every small town. A bigger problem occurred when restaurateurs started to pocket more money by using lesser-quality products, lowering the quality of the food. It was not until the Velvet Revolution in 1989, when the Communist Party collapsed, that the Czech National Culinary Team started to participate in various food competitions. Most of the time they ended up taking fifteenth or sixteenth place in world competitions. Certainly that was because the taste was there, but the presentation needed to improve for Czech gastronomy to regain the reputation it had once held alongside the cuisines of Paris and Vienna.

The Return to Glory

Today, the Czech National Culinary Team receives gold, silver, and bronze medals in international competitions for taste and presentation. Bravo! As Czech cuisine now returns to its former glory, I am proud to showcase the national Czech food that we call: *Staročeská kuchyně* or "Recipes of our grandmothers." This type of cooking was unbelievably modest, yet it was nourishing, sustainable, and had incredible layers of flavor. With its endurance through eras of prosperity and want, Czech cuisine incorporates values of thrift and conservation, and teaches the skill of bringing robust flavor from nothing to make miracles.

My Life in Prague

If you were told to "meet under the horse's tail," most Czechs would know that there is only one place in the world to meet. It is Wenceslas Square in Prague—the place where I grew up. The statue of the Good King Wenceslas, the patron of Bohemia, proudly sits on his bronze horse. This symbolic square that plays such an important role in the history of Prague was my backyard.

Down on the square, I would hopscotch on cobblestones, jumping on the blue ones and skipping the white ones. It was the fountain in front of the National Museum where I would dip my white, Sunday-best gloves. It always upset my dear mother. I loved this fountain. I grew up at my mother's side in downtown restaurants. Day by day watching her, learning from her, and weighing ingredients for her recipes when she became legally blind, I unknowingly absorbed the knowledge of what goes where, how much, and for how long it cooks.

It was here, in my mother's restaurant located on the sixth floor of the Bata shoe store building, where I would watch the Communist party's parades.

I was here in August of 1968, when all the citizens of Prague tried to stop the Soviet invasion and their tanks and a year later when Jan Palach committed self-immolation in the name of liberty.

I was here in 1972, when the Czechs won the World Cup in ice hockey against the Russians. It was a memorable occasion. Immediately after the conclusion of the game, my mother dragged me into the square where Czechs gathered in jubilation.

During my teen years, I walked from my home, down Wenceslas Square, to the Civil Engineering School, realizing how beautiful the architecture of Prague was. Among these were: the beautiful National Museum built in neo-renaissance style; the Koruna Palace, which reflects the influence of eastern civilization with its Babylonian style; and the Grand Hotel Europa in the art nouveau style; the Lucerna Palace, the place where I took dancing lessons and attended my prom. All the other buildings with decorations and frescoes on the facades explain the history of the Czech people.

I was very active in sports. I was most successful in rowing. In the years 1971–1975, I became a seven-time champion on the Czech rowing team in 4s and 8s. We competed outside of Czechoslovakia, many times in

Denise rowing, age sixteen. She is in the far boat facing the coxswain.

Denise at six years old in Prague.

Eastern Germany. It was in 1975 when our coach told us the news that the year 1976 would be the first year when women would to be able to compete in the Olympic games in Montreal. At the same time, I graduated from the Civil Engineering School in Prague and obtained a bachelor's degree, still rowing in the afternoons and evenings.

I had a remarkable childhood but was destined to leave the country that I loved because I did not fit Communist cookie-cutter politics. My boss at work had to pick one person out of our office to join the Communist Party. Unfortunately, he thought I was the best pick—young, full of energy, and enthusiastic. That day when he announced this news was a black day for me. I was devastated. I did not want to be involved in the party. Communism had taken everything that my parents had worked for all their lives. I did not know what to do. Everything in my life seemed to have come to an end.

Rather than join the Communist Party, I defected in 1976 at the age of nineteen. After a long struggle to obtain a visa, I purchased an airline ticket marked "Prague–Frankfurt" and a train ticket marked "Frankfurt–Baden-Baden–Paris." I thought that eventually going to Montreal would be an excellent idea since I spoke French. The second I arrived in Paris, before any sightseeing or anything else, I looked up the Canadian Embassy and applied for asylum.

Political Asylum

There were lots of happy times for me in Paris. I worked at the Hotel Concord Lafayette. Unfortunately, after eighteen months the immigration office wrote me a letter telling me that my reasons for having left Czechoslovakia were not political and that they were not good enough. Therefore, they asked that I leave France immediately. Leave France? Go back to Czechoslovakia? I would end up in jail! The Canadian Embassy informed me at this same time that the Canadian government was not accepting any more immigrants. Now what?

Through the Czech underground immigration office in Paris, I was informed that there was a possibility that I could go to the United States of America. I would have to get myself to Munich, answer some questions and wait—wait for the future. I really did not have other choices. My escape from France to Germany was more dramatic than my move from Communist Prague to Paris. The French would not give me a visa to leave, and they would not give me permits to stay.

Fortunately, I met a man who was able to give me a fake passport with directions of what to do. I had to purchase a couchette train ticket Paris-Munich, and I had to perfectly learn answers in French without an accent. What is your name? (actually, somebody else) What is your nationality? Where are you going to and why? With one suitcase (and believe me, that was very hard to reduce all my belongings in to one suitcase), I had to leave beautiful clothes behind me and keep only a few of my dearest things.

I remember it like it was yesterday. I remember that I had a little bit of wine to ease my nerves. I wore a two-piece beige French couture outfit. At the ticket window

Denise's mother, Jarmila Resnerová Pášová, second from left in front row.

in the train station, I asked where my train was departing from. Once I was inside the train, I really did not want to start any conversations with anybody because they would find out that I had an accent. I immediately jumped into my bed in my clothes and prayed. A few minutes later the train conductor came and asked for the tickets and passports. I did my job answering all the necessary questions, and Mr. Conductor wished me a good night's sleep. I tried to fall asleep, but so many possible things were going through my mind. Am I going to wake up in Munich or in prison? The next morning when the train started to slow down, I woke up. The sun was about to rise when I found the strength to look outside the window.

I saw name of the city written in the German language and started to cry. I knew that I was going to be okay. When we arrived in Munich, Mr. Conductor returned my passport with a smile. I just replied, "Merci beaucoup!" I do not believe he knew. I was so happy. I felt a presence in my heart that everything was wide open.

My mother was able to come to see me in Munich, Germany, before I left the Old World to an unknown future. The day I picked her up from the train station she had this huge, old leather bag filled with a still-warm roasted duck, dumplings, and sauerkraut. Bless her heart. The food smelled amazing and was delicious. As we spoke, she warned me, "Denise, you closed your doors, and don't ever come home." It must have been so hard for her to say that. First, she was robbed by the Communists when they took her pension away, and now, she was losing her daughter.

As we talked some more, she told me how the police officer in Prague was frequently visiting her and made her to promise that she would try to convince me to come back. They had been saying that nothing would happen to me. She knew that this was a lie. We spent a couple of days together, and when she left, she gave me her blessings.

Soon after that I got a message from the immigration officer in Germany that I had been offered work for the Belgium Ambassador in Aspen, Colorado, as a housekeeper and cook. I accepted. My departure was scheduled for October 31, 1978.

Starting Over in the United States

Arrival in New York was very intimidating. "New York, USA," words people would only whisper in Czechoslovakia. When I arrived in Denver, Colorado, a friend suggested that before going to Aspen, I stop by Boulder where there were some Czech people. I received the address of a gentleman whose father was working for a Czech radio station in 1968 and had to run right after the invasion. She called him to arrange a visit. Mr. C. was very accepting. He listened to my long story of how I had gotten to Boulder, and then he said, "Let's go to the café so you can meet more people." The next morning, we went to the café. A short rambunctious lady greeted us, "Welcome, sit down, sit down. Would you like coffee?

"*Ano*," I replied. She smiled and then sat down too. We talked and talked. Her husband worked as a professor at the university and said he knew some people in the civil engineering department and that perhaps I could apply for work there. I applied at the university, but there was the problem of language. I did not know how to speak English. Mary, the owner of the Czech restaurant offered me a job. She said, "Denise, you can peel potatoes, and I will pay you $1.00 per hour."

You must be kidding! I thought. Me, an executive employee of the Charles University will peel potatoes for $1.00 per hour? Then I suddenly realized that I was here in my new home to stay forever. Not knowing any English, I decided to start totally from the bottom. I accepted the job. The first day it took me one and a half hours to peel two big buckets of potatoes. I earned $1.50. The following day I was asked to come at 6:00 a.m., and the owner showed me how she made kolaches, pancakes, and waffle dough. After just a few days of working in the restaurant, I became a baker, a prep cook, and a line chef. I was good at making soups—gallons and gallons of soup! Homemade breads, apple strudels, chocolate roulades, schnitzels with potato salad, chicken paprika, roast pork, dumplings, and kraut. My love for cooking became my way of breathing. Growing up with a mother who was a chef, I knew how hard it was to work in the kitchens, and my mother didn't want me to work as hard as she did. By getting a degree in civil engineering, I had tried to stay away from restaurants, but cooking is my passion, and throughout my exile in the United States I have always ended up in kitchens. I had a job paying me below minimum wage, but I was happy. I could speak Czech there, and I was adding new English words every day.

I was working in the café in the mornings six days a week, and I was always looking for some more work in the afternoons. I found a job as a bus girl in a very nice, stylish restaurant whose owner used to come to our café for a late lunch. Waiting on tables was a good transformation for me. I had to speak to people, and that helped me to excel in English. I worked from 6:00 a.m. till 2:30 p.m. as a chef and then started my second job as a waitress at 4:30 and stayed there until closing at 10:00 p.m. or later, depending on how long our customers would stay. Between jobs I rested by the pool at my friend's apartment complex and would fall asleep under a tree for an hour. I survived living like this for thirteen months. I saved enough of money to make the down payment for brand-new town house. I made lots of friends in Boulder. I met my husband in Boulder and started our family there.

The Texas Hill Country

Later, we moved to San Antonio, Texas. When I moved to the Hill Country of Texas, I wanted to open a restaurant, but still carrying the words of my mother, who discouraged me from working in restaurants, and wanting to be able to spend time with my four young children, I chose to open a knitting shop. I have always liked to knit. At my school in Prague, I would knit vigorously under my desk all the time. In Paris I would knit sweaters and sell them to the waiters working at the Au Fouquet Restaurant on the Champs-Elyssées. Knitting was a little refuge and freedom from the ordinary day. Knitting had carried me through civil engineering school and helped me to stay focused before every rowing competition. With two knitting needles in my hands, I defected from Czechoslovakia. Knitting needles built a bridge between insanity of political asylum in France and freedom in the USA. The knitting shop was a wonderful journey in my life, definitely a great stepping stone: learning about marketing, customer service, and displaying; finding merchandise that would be different from other stores; creating and publishing my patterns in Vogue Knitting magazine; making contracts with international suppliers in the Czech Republic, Germany, and France; paying bills; and planning.

I learned how to speak English better by teaching others how to knit. Over twenty years of teaching, I tried to find a guide for my students to re-emphasize what I had taught, and because I could not find such a source, I decided to write the book *Knitting the Continental Way*, which teaches how to crochet and knit step-by-step (Author House, 2016).

Hosting knitting circles and listening to my customers, I realized that my shop had become a destination for people from all over San Antonio, all the surroundings in

My, velmistři a mistři našich cechů, pod patronaci svatého Vavřince, na slavnostnim sezeni vydati ráčime tento historický

Pasovaci list velmistra

Tímto certifikátem veřejně známo činime že:

Pan: Denise Mazal

dokázal, že je schopen připravit krmně a piti pro vladaře, jež odstrani hněv a chmury z jeho čela, vyjasní jeho myst, nastoli pokoru a pochopení pro spravedlivé posouzeni věci, o kterých musi rozhodnout.

Měj stále na paměti, že svůj um musiš dál rozvijet, svědomi své slovem a činem zlým nikdy nezatěžuj, a naše regule a dobré české zvyky, tradice a obyčeje zachovávej, abys všem cechům svatého Vavřince jen ku prospěchu byl.

Svým podpisem stvrzuji: velmistr.

mistr.

Sepsáno a zapečetěno v den pasování

Léta páně v obci: 23. 10. 2010

Uděluje Československý svaz kuchařů v Praze

předseda:

We, the Grandmasters and Masters of our culinary guilds, under the auspices of Saint Vavřinec, on this festive occasion, we are pleased to issue this historical

DIPLOMA

By this Certification, let it be known that:

Ms. Denise Mazal

Proved to be able to prepare food and drinks for the Royalty to smooth their wrath and sadness, to clear their minds, restore their humility and sense of justice about matters they must decide upon.

Be aware, to develop your craft still further and never to burden your conscience with evil word or deed; keep in mind fairness, our good Czech customs and traditions always for the benefit of all Czechs of Saint Vavřinec.

We hereby affix our signatures: Grandmaster: Jaroslav Sapik

Master: Jiři Král

Signed and sealed on this date of issuance:

On this day of our Lord, October 23, 2010

Granted by the Association of Czechoslovak Chefs in Prague

Chairman: Jaroslav Sapik

Hill Country as far as Houston. They all had been asking about a food that would represent Boerne's and my heritage. Good German food and Czech kolaches.

It hurt to hear people saying that the only kolaches sold in gas stations are not real kolaches but klobasniky, sausage wrapped in dough. And the kolaches with fruit fillings at other stores are not at all how they remember when their grandmother made them. I had to agree that real, true kolaches do not exist in stores in the USA. Information about kolaches was very limited on the internet, saying that kolaches are Polish. I still thought about my mother's warnings about the difficulties of working in a restaurant, but I was determined that one day a Czech restaurant would be born.

In 2000, I took out a loan and built a restaurant next door to my knitting shop and began searching for a restauranteur who could help me. In one of my trips to Prague in 2003, I met Chef Jan Michalek (at that time the manager of a Czech culinary team), to whom I expressed the need of a Czech restaurant in Texas. He liked the idea and said, "Once you have your restaurant, let me know, and I will come."

In 2005 my mother metaphorically gave me the green light to open my restaurant. At the age of ninety, she wanted to come to United States and bake kolaches to sell. I had an airline ticket for her to come, all her belongings packed in a thirty-six-foot container on a big ship. But on September 11, 2005, she passed away.

I used my experience working side-by-side with my mother and in European hotels and restaurants to design a floor plan, choose the equipment, and create a business plan. It took three more years after my mother's death for it all to come together. I opened the restaurant Little Gretel with my daughter Veronica in late January 2009. The restaurant offered Central European cuisine such as Authentic Czech, Traditional German, and added American favorites.

Special Honors

2010
Best Business of the Year, by Greater Chamber of Commerce, Boerne, Texas.

2013
Best Chefs America. The top 1% of chefs in the United States receive this prestige award.

2015
Best Businesswoman, by Greater Boerne Chamber of Commerce, Boerne, Texas.

2018-2019
Women Business Owner Award, by NAWBO, San Antonio, finalist.

2021
Best 15 Small Town Restaurants across the US, by Travel Awaits, finalist.

May 15, 2023
I officially announced my retirement.

"Thank you for recognizing Little Gretel as not just 'another restaurant' but a special place to dine, a place where through all your senses, you could experience my stories and where you could see firsthand that Czech cuisine is right there, competing with the other cuisines of the world."

Little Gretel

Little Gretel became an instant success, serving everything from breakfast and brunch to lunch, dinner, and desserts. Diners loved the sauerkraut, schnitzels, chicken paprika, meatloaf, roasted duck, and of course, kolaches, fruit dumplings, apple strudel, and more. Everything was made from scratch, in house at Little Gretel.

Chef Jan Michalek joined us with Chef Vaclav Pstros and Pastry Chef Lukas Skala for couple of weeks in October. Our focus was to bring to the table wild game, which was served for special occasions in Czech Republic. The Texas Hill Country has ample wild game. I learn how to not only prepare the meat but how to butcher whole animals and use all the cuts from nose to tail.

These types of yearly visits became very popular and festive. Bobie Rawitz, former owner of the iconic Yarn Barn of San Antonio, visited us one day, and told me that Little Gretel set a trend for Boerne because nothing like this was created here before. I treasured her words for very long time.

Success brought more responsibilities. Staying two steps ahead from everybody else in town made me be even more creative. We started to serve dinners with a theme. We took guests on journeys all over the world with authentic menus of each country. The most memorable dinner was the "Last Dinner on the Titanic," on April 14, 2012, one hundred years after the ship sank. The atmosphere of the Titanic voyage was brilliantly presented. Red carpet in the entrance, tables decorated with crystal chandeliers, guests coming in glamorous dresses of that era, and of course, music playing from Puccini and Tchaikovsky. The food was exceptional. I practiced the recipes from the Great Liner for weeks. It took me about three weeks to create the Titanic ship out of Jello!

The word about my cooking spread overseas. On October 23rd, 2010, I received a certification, in the form of a diploma granted by the Association of Czechoslovak Chefs in Prague, sign by Grandmaster Jaroslav Sapik and Master Jiri Kral. Receiving this recognition was proof of my ability to prepare food fit for royalty.

Aromas and Memories

I measure my cooking achievements by the intensity of scent memories it creates.

I love the smell of rain. I love the smell of the sun on a meadow, and I can see the meadow by the railroad where I walked with my mother as she pointed out juniper berries, saying, "This berry is good in every dish when cooking a forest animal."

I love that scents can bring memories back to life.

My favorite smell is the aroma of a Sunday morning. I close my eyes, and in that moment, I see an open window where the wind moves the white lacy curtains. I hear from far away the gentle music of Antonín Dvořák, and when I step closer to the window, I can smell competing aromas from all the other open windows. Of course, the smell of my mother's freshly baked apple strudel was always the winner.

Tips for Success

1. Invest in a good scale which converts from ounces to grams instantly. You will love it! When you cook, the weight can be approximate, but when you bake you have to be accurate! It is much easier to weigh 50 grams of butter than 3 tablespoons of butter, especially when you use top quality butter, which has no tablespoon marks.

2. The first and most important secret I will reveal right now is that when I refer to "Kosher salt," I mean that you will use Diamond Crystal salt. This salt sticks to the foods, therefore you need less of it, and you know that less salty is better for your health. It dissolves quickly (about twice as fast as table salt), and you'll be able to quickly decide if you need to add more or not. On the other hand, Morton table salt has a different structure and is twice as salty by volume as Diamond Crystal salt. If you are going to be using table salt, make sure you adjust the amount.

3. Follow your heart! Connect with the meal you are creating. Use wooden spoons instead of metal for stirring. Wooden spoons don't heat as fast, they don't scratch the bottoms of pots, and they don't chemically react with acids. Using wooden spoons connect you with your food in a way that metal spoons don't. They transfer your happy intentions into the food.

Czech food is a hidden gem. It is very old, very healthy, and will inspire a new generation. Some of its unique value is in the way the food is prepared, which I share throughout this book. This cookbook will be enjoyed by anyone who loves to cook good homemade food from scratch, those who have a passion for good food, and those who would like to expand their knowledge of central European cooking. I hope that this book will bring joy and that you will often reach for it for inspiration.

Taste of Homeland

The article below describes the first visit of my dear friends and colleagues from Prague, to whom I give big credit. The article was written for the *Boerne Star* newspaper in 2009, soon after we opened the restaurant.

Taste of Homeland
Czech chefs to visit Little Gretel
By Elena Tucker
Staff Writer

Twenty-five years ago, Denise Mazal arrived in Boerne after a long and complicated journey that began with defection from her beloved but then Communist Czech Republic.

The six-year adventure that eventually brought her to the Hill Country involved false identity papers, clandestine train rides, a failed bid for French asylum, escape to Germany, and eventual invitation to the United States. "I went through everything," Mazal said. But when she arrived in Boerne—and more specifically, set sight on the property she eventually purchased on River Road—Mazal said it was "love at first sight."

Now, with this year's opening of her Little Gretel restaurant, Chef Mazal has merged her love for Prague with that of her adopted home. Next month, Mazal's eatery will host an event that the restaurateur expects will both broaden and deepen those ties. From Nov. 15–23, three visiting Czech chefs will simultaneously descend upon Little Gretel.

"They will actually cook with me in the kitchen—showing me things," Mazal said. "I want to bring my food to a higher level. It's a cooking school for me that I want to share with others."

Mazal will be joined in the kitchen by long-time friend and executive chef Jan Michalek, as well as pastry specialist Lukas Skala and grilling master Vaclav Pstros.

While Mazal plans to learn from the visiting chefs, she also looks forward to watching them "compete" with one another for customers' favor. Diners will be included in the event since they're to be asked for feedback. "Patrons will be ordering, eating, and I will be asking, Which did you like the best? Mazal said. "I really hope to see joy in the patrons' eyes."

By offering her Czech cuisine to Boerne customers, Mazal gives them a taste of their own German heritage. Czech and German foods have borrowed so heavily from each other over the centuries as to be practically indistinguishable, according to Mazal.

"We eat exactly the same things," the chef said, although concluding, "maybe Germans use a little bit more juniper and clove in their sauerkraut—I don't do that."

Most anticipated of all is the camaraderie that the Little Gretel owner knows she'll enjoy in the kitchen, side by side with other chefs who share her love both for

Little Gretel Restaurant

the homeland and for familiar cooking traditions. The undertones will be deep, Mazal said, since citizens of oppressed Eastern Block countries such as hers learned to communicate in ways besides just words.

"The food can have hidden secrets," Mazal said with visible enthusiasm regarding the upcoming culinary event. Whatever the guest chefs bring to Little Gretel, it won't be the first time Prague's food has come to visit Mazal. During her troubled time in Munich, communist officials unexpectedly allowed Mazal's mother, an acclaimed Czech chef herself, to leave the country for a trip to Germany.

"She came and I picked her up at the train station," Mazal said. "There she was with a huge leather bag and there was—still hot—roasted duck with sauerkraut and dumplings. I mean, imagine! I said, 'How did they let you go with this food?' And she said, 'Denise, you don't understand—I'm here on a mission. They want me to convince you to come back. But you know, you closed the door behind you and you cannot come back. Ever.'"

But Mazal did go back in 1993 after the wall came down, and several times more she's returned to the Czech Republic—always taking a piece of Boerne with her. Now for a change, her homeland will come to Mazal in the form of three countrymen. Though they're not likely to woo her back to Prague with a suitcase of roast duck and dumplings, they are certain to bring a taste of long-ago home to Denise Mazal, who'll be sharing her Little Gretel kitchen with them for nine November days.

Recipes

1 Appetizers

Předkrmy

When I hear the word "appetizer" I hear "appetite teaser" . . . and yes, that's what it is.

An appetizer is a dish that is served before a main meal. Its purpose is not to fill you up but to encourage the senses and, especially, to lift expectations of other food to come. This intensifies the experience of the next course served.

Czech appetizers in the form of pâtés, gelatines, and terrines have been served as main courses in our nation for a thousand years. Today these dishes are served mostly as appetizers or snacks.

Pâté originated in northern and central Europe cuisines. In the Middle Ages, it was a staple—an economical and flavorful way to use all of the animal. Czechs are very proud of their *paštika* (pâté). It is a must for picnics and sandwiches when you travel. Pâtés are made of liver, and the basic mixture is usually fine and spreadable. Terrines are generally made out of chunkier pieces of meat cooked in a deep mold and served in slices.

Gelatines and aspics are clear savory jellies made out of thickened meat broth cooled in a mold. They are served cold in slices.

Asparagus with Ham and Hollandaise Sauce

Chřest se Šunkou a Holandskou Omáčkou

Czech asparagus was esteemed as the best, not only in Austria, but all over Europe.

4-6 SERVINGS

1 pound (450 grams) green asparagus

1 pound (450 grams) white asparagus

½ pound (225 grams) ham, thinly sliced

Diamond Crystal Kosher salt, for cooking asparagus

10 tablespoons (140 grams) unsalted butter

3 egg yolks

1 teaspoon (5 grams) cold water

Pinch of Diamond Crystal Kosher salt

1 tablespoon (14 grams) lemon juice

1 tablespoon (7 grams) scallions, sliced

HOLLANDAISE SAUCE:

- Melt butter in a measuring cup (with spout).
- Skim the separated milk foam from the top.
- At the same time, mix egg yolks in food processor.
- Add salt and cold water.
- Slowly drizzle melted butter into the food processor, making sure that the cloudy white milk residue settled on the bottom doesn't get into your sauce.
- Add lemon juice.
- In a skillet with butter, warm up slices of ham.

TO SERVE arrange the spears of the asparagus on a plate; spoon hollandaise sauce over parts of the spears, place sliced warm ham on top, and sprinkle with sliced scallions.

TIP *When butter is heated, it splits into three components. Floating foam on the top, white milky liquid on the bottom. Clear yellow liquid in the middle is clarified butter. Clarified butter is what you use to make Hollandaise sauce.*

Drowned Sausages

Utopenci

This popular Czech dish is Speck Sausages pickled in a sweet and sour tangy marinade with bay leaves, onions, red bell pepper, and spices. It has been a staple of Czech cuisine for over one hundred years and is traditionally served in pubs with bread and beer. The legendary dish is believed to have been invented by a pub owner and miller when he was trying to preserve sausages for long periods before refrigeration was available. The name of the dish—*Utopenec* (*Utopenci* is plural)—was inspired by the tragic death of the owner, who drowned while he was fixing the wheel on his mill. The fact that sausages are "drowning" in marinade can also explain the name.

8 SERVINGS

Ingredients for Marinade:

1 quart (1 liter) water

2 cups (450 milliliters) vinegar

2 tablespoons (30 grams) sugar

1 teaspoon (3 grams) Diamond Crystal Kosher salt

1 teaspoon (4 grams) black ground pepper

6 whole allspice berries

⅛ teaspoon (1 gram) cayenne pepper

5 bay leaves

2 stems of lovage (use Italian parsley if you don't have lovage)

2 stems of dill

Ingredients for each glass jar with sausages:

8 Homemade Speck Sausages

1 small yellow onion, sliced

1 red bell pepper, sliced

2 large dill pickles, sliced

5 cloves of garlic

3 small bay leaves

2 stems of dill

1 gallon glass jar with lid

Cooking twine for tying the sausages

DIRECTIONS FOR SAUSAGES:

- Peel off casings and butterfly the sausages lengthwise.
- Stuff each sausage with onion, bell pepper, and pickles, and secure the stuffing with cooking twine.
- Place the stuffed sausages into a large glass jar. Add garlic, bay leaf, and dill.
- Fill the jar with hot marinade.
- Close and let rest upside down in the refrigerator for 2 weeks.

Homemade Speck Sausages

Domací Špekáčky

Špekáčky have received a protected EU designation. The European Commission has added Czech Speck Sausages to the list of Traditional Specialties Guaranteed. It means that this kind of sausage originated in Czech lands and demonstrates the traditional method of production and composition.

These smoked sausages are the basic ingredient in the Drowned Sausages recipe.

5 pounds (2,250 grams) beef, ground

3 pounds (1,400 grams) pork, about 80% lean / 20% fat

2 pounds (900 grams) pork fatback, small diced

2 teaspoons (14 grams) pink curing salt (Prague #1 or Insta Cure #1)

3 tablespoons (27 grams) garlic, minced

¼ cup (45 grams) Diamond Crystal Kosher salt

3 tablespoons (25 grams) ground white pepper

3 tablespoons (20 grams) Hungarian paprika

2 teaspoons (6 grams) grated nutmeg

2 cups (500 milliliters) cold water

- Grind beef and pork into a mixing bowl.
- Add salts, garlic, pepper, paprika, and nutmeg, and mix all together with your hands.
- Add cold water and continue to mix all into a fine mixture.
- Add diced pork fatback; mix.
- Let it rest for 24 hours in the refrigerator.
- Using a sausage maker, make 4-inch-long wursts (10 centimeters long).
- Place dry wursts into a smoker and smoke for 20 minutes.
- Cook in hot water over low heat for 45 minutes. Water temperature should be about 160° F (70° C).

TIP *I highly recommend using Camerons Stovetop Smoker. It is amazingly easy and not messy.*

Prague Ham

After many years of relative obscurity, Prague Ham (*Pražská Šunka*) has finally gained international recognition. This traditional Czech delicacy has been added to the EU list of so-called Traditional Specialties Guaranteed.

This delicacy was created by Prague butcher and smoker Frantisek Zverina, who in 1857 invented the initial method: curing, smoking, and then cooking a whole pork leg. At the time of its creation, none of the manufacturers took care of its trademark or other protection. The particular taste of this ham enchanted customers, and soon major cities in the Austrian-Hungarian Empire began to emulate the process, and it began to be produced in Vienna, Budapest, France, Italy, and the United States. Today Prague Ham is still very popular around the world.

The Belgians defend Ardennes Ham and follow a process of marinating and smoking meat that has hardly changed for centuries. Spaniards are proud of Jamon Iberico, a dried ham from black Iberian pigs. The Germans protect the process for Schwarzwalder Schinken, a ham from the Black Forest. Italians are proud of their famous Prosciutto di Parma, originated in the province of Parma. But the fact is that the method of making ham was created by a Czech!

Pink Salt for Curing the Sausages

Prague #1 (there is also Prague #2) with its nickname "Pragovka" is used in meat processing. This pink salt pulls the water out of bacteria cells and kills them. Prague powder #1 is especially effective in preventing the growth of the deadly clostridium botulinum bacteria, which causes botulism.

Ham Cones filled with Horseradish Whipped Cream

Šunkové Kornouty plněné Křenovou Šlehačkou

While in many places in the world, baguettes and sandwiches are leading on-the-go items, the Czechs like to sit down and forget about the world while they get carried away with beautiful, elaborate appetizers.

It was Paukert's delicatessen in 1916 in Prague who introduced us to these festive appetizers.

4-6 SERVINGS

8 pieces ham, sliced

1 cup (250 milliliters) heavy cream

½ cup (125 grams) fresh horseradish, finely grated

Pinch of Diamond Crystal Kosher salt

1 red bell pepper, sliced

8 rosettes of fresh parsley

8 black olives, sliced

- Whip heavy cream with salt to a peak.
- Fold in grated horseradish.
- Form cones from the ham and pipe horseradish whipped cream inside of cones.
- Decorate the cones with slices of red bell pepper, black olives, and snips of parsley.

Carrot Marmalade

Mrkvová Marmeláda

Czechs are known for making marmalades using fruit they grow in their gardens or pick in the forests. They also make vegetable marmalades.

MAKES TWO 16-OUNCE JARS

8 cups (900 grams) carrots, peeled and grated

1 cup (250 milliliters) water

1 cup (200 grams) sugar

Orange peel from 1 orange

¼ cup (60 grams) fresh-squeezed orange juice

¼ cup (60 grams) fresh-squeezed lemon juice

1 pinch of Diamond Crystal Kosher salt

- In a pot, on medium-high heat, cook carrots and orange peel in water until they are tender, about 30 minutes. Stir occasionally. If water evaporates and carrots are not cooked yet, add a little more water.
- When carrots are tender, add sugar and salt.
- Remove the orange peel. Blend the mixture with a stick (immersion) blender.
- Add lemon and orange juice, and cook until the marmalade thickens.
- Pour the hot marmalade into sealed, sterilized glass jars, and let it cool in the refrigerator upside down.

Aspic

Aspik

The perfect dish for a summer day! If you enjoy making broth and drinking it as a beverage, you will discover that aspic is a very healthy and refreshing dish on a hot summer day. It is gelatinized cold soup with meat and vegetables.

4-6 SERVINGS

½ quart (500 milliliters) ham hock stock

½ pound (200 grams) ham hock meat, small diced

2 hard-boiled eggs, sliced

1 cup (130 grams) frozen green peas, defrosted

1 cup (128 grams) carrots, cooked, medium diced

1 can (28 ounces / 500 grams) of fire-roasted red peppers

4 packages gelatin

Pinch of Diamond Crystal Kosher salt

Black ground pepper

Distilled white vinegar

Onions, finely sliced

2 molds (4 x 8 inches)

- Make ham hock stock.
- Strain the liquid from ham hock.
- Peel all the meat of the ham hock from the bones and dice it.
- Add gelatin to the liquid according to the instruction on the gelatin label. Season it with salt and pepper to the taste. Stir.
- Grease a mold and place slices of hard-boiled egg on the bottom. Then add diced ham hock meat, peas, carrots, and sliced roasted red peppers.
- Pour gelatin–ham hock liquid over the mixture, and let it cool in the refrigerator.
- When gelatin is solid, the aspic is ready for serving.

SERVE on a plate, place a slice of aspic, sprinkle with diced onions, and drizzle with vinegar.

This recipe will be handy when you have saved extra bones from T-bone steaks, pork ribs, or any other cuts of meat that you would normally throw away.

Duck Confit

Konfitovaná Kachna

The confit is a process of preservation that consists of salt-curing a piece of meat and later cooking it in its own fat. This effortless technique guarantees the best result: tender and perfectly juicy!

One half of Duck Confit is used to make Duck Rillettes.

2 SERVINGS

1 whole duck

3 tablespoons (30 grams) Diamond Crystal Kosher salt

2 tablespoons (30 grams) garlic, roughly chopped

3 large star anise, ground

Pinch of cinnamon, ground

1 tablespoon (10 grams) ginger, minced

Zest from 1 orange

½ cup (50 grams) carrot marmalade (optional)

8 black peppercorns, crushed

1 stem rosemary, fresh

4 cups (800 grams) rendered duck fat, divided

- Rinse the duck thoroughly.
- Cut off the wings, neck skin, and the tail.
- Cut the duck in half lengthwise and remove the spine. Split the breast from the leg. Save all the scraps for a stock.
- Rub the duck all over with mixture of the salt, garlic, star anise, cinnamon, ginger, orange zest, carrot marmalade (optional), peppercorns, and rosemary.
- Cover the duck with two cups of rendered duck fat, then cover with plastic wrap.
- Refrigerate overnight.
- Preheat oven to 200° F (95° C).
- Pour off the rendered fat and rinse the duck under cold water. Wipe off all the seasoning.
- Place the pieces of duck in a roasting pot and cover pieces completely with the two remaining (fresh) cups of rendered duck fat.
- Place the pot, uncovered, in the oven and cook for 5-6 hours, or until the duck is completely tender.
- Strain juice. Save juices for later use. Set aside the pieces of meat.
- Refrigerate the pieces you will not use immediately together with unused juices.

ENJOY half of the duck as a main dish, and use the other half for Duck Rillettes.

Duck Rillettes

Kachní Rillettes

Rillettes are tender, shredded pieces of seasoned meat that can be served over salad or on a piece of toast. The texture is loose, with threads of visible meat, and it can be stored for later use in containers covered with fat. It is a very good way to preserve duck meat for later use.

2 SERVINGS

½ cup (125 grams) of gelatinized juice from duck

1 tablespoon (15 milliliters) cognac or brandy

Zest from half an orange

1 tablespoon (4 grams) fresh parsley, chopped

Pinch of Diamond Crystal Kosher salt and pepper to taste

Solidified duck fat from top of gelatinized juices

1 tablespoon (6 grams) scallions, sliced for decoration

Cornichons

Bread, fried

- Take the other half of the duck confit out of the roasting pan. Discard the skin and bones. Scrape solidified fat from top of gelatinized juices, and set aside.
- With your fingers, break all the meat into small pieces.
- Adjust the seasoning with salt, pepper, and add 1 tablespoon of solidified duck fat. Stir.
- In a sauté pan, heat up reserved gelatinized juice, cognac or brandy, zest from orange, and parsley. Stir.
- Pour this mixture over rillettes and stir. Let cool.
- Place rillettes into small jars and cover them with reserved solidified duck fat.
- At this stage, you can store rillettes in the refrigerator for up to 1 month.

SERVE the rillettes as a spread over fried bread. Garnish with cornichons or any other pickled vegetables. Sprinkle with scallions or roll them into a taco.

TIP *Duck fat is high in beneficial monounsaturated and polyunsaturated fat. Its chemical composition is closer to olive oil than to butter. Its resistance to breaking down at high temperatures makes it a better choice than most other oils. Duck fat is wonderful for frying potatoes, and searing and roasting meats. The results are richer taste and improved texture.*

Liver Pâté

Játrová Pomazánka

This is an easy recipe that will make you stand out at party!

6-8 SERVINGS

1 pound (450 grams) chicken liver, well-trimmed, cut into 1-inch pieces

1 cup (227 grams) unsalted butter

½ cup (75 grams) onion, chopped

1 bay leaf

½ teaspoon (2 grams) dried thyme

¼ cup (60 milliliters) red wine

1 teaspoon brandy

Pinch of Diamond Crystal Kosher salt and black pepper

bread, fried in butter or oil

- Melt ¼ cup butter in skillet over medium heat.
- Add onions and bay leaf. Sauté until onions are translucent.
- Add chicken liver, thyme, and red wine, and sauté until liver is tender, about 8–10 minutes. Do not overcook. Liver should be pinkish but not bloody. Do not add salt yet; salt will make the liver hard.
- Discard bay leaf.
- In a food processor, combine cooled sautéed liver mixture with ¾ cup butter, brandy, salt, and pepper.
- Fill small glass jars with the pâté and let them cool.

SERVE pâté as a spread over fried bread.

TIP *To save pâté for later use, cover top of pâté with a thin layer of melted butter.*

Steak Tartar

Tatarský Biftek

A very popular dish in Czech restaurants is Steak Tartar, fresh, minced raw beef with a myriad of ingredients served around the plate. How much of each ingredient to add is up to each guest! You mix it to taste, and become your own chef. It is served with fried bread (*Topinka*) smeared with fresh garlic.

4 SERVINGS

28 ounces (800 grams) beef tenderloin, cubed, or lean top sirloin without fat or gristle

4 egg yolks, 1 for each person

Bread, fried in butter or oil

4 tablespoons (36 grams) garlic, minced

Yellow mustard

Ketchup

Worcestershire sauce

4 tablespoons (30-50 grams) onions, finely chopped

Cayenne pepper

Red paprika

Diamond crystal kosher salt

Black pepper

Whole egg for creating the indentation

- Grind cold cubed beef in meat grinder twice.
- Form four 7-ounce (200 grams) balls.
- Flatten the top with your fingers, and with whole egg make an indentation in the middle.
- Add yolk inside this indentation.

SERVE:

- On a large plate or wooden board, center the Steak Tartar and surround it with the chopped onion, minced garlic, and all the dry spices in separate small piles.
- Serve liquid condiments inside small glass jars.

YOU AS A CHEF:

- Using a fork, mix the meat and egg on your plate with onions and garlic.
- Add mustard, ketchup, salt, cayenne pepper, black pepper, and red paprika. Add spices to your taste.
- Spread the Steak Tartar over fried bread.

Pork Caviar Milos Forman

Škvarky pro Miloše Formana

Pork Caviar was Miloš Forman's favorite snack. (He was the director of many award-winning movies—*One Flew Over the Cuckoo's Nest, Amadeus, The People vs. Larry Flynt, Man on the Moon, Ragtime, Hair,* etc.) He used to call my friend Chef Václav saying: "I'll be in Prague tomorrow. Could you make me Pork Caviar?" And indeed, my friend would make it and deliver it to the airport.

10-12 SERVINGS

1½ pound (680 grams) pork belly fat, preferably only fat, no meat

½ cup (120 milliliters) cold water

½ cup (120 milliliters) milk

- Cut pork fat into ½-inch squares.
- Add both pork fat and cold water to a skillet.
- Place the skillet over medium-low heat. You don't want to see smoke of any kind. Once the temperature is right, you'll notice small bubbles. Do not cover.
- The lard will render slowly. The whole process will take about 1½ hours. Stir to prevent sticking. Do not rush.
- Some pieces of fat will cook faster than others. Remove these cracklings as soon as you see them and place them to the side so that they will not burn.
- When there is a lot of fat but the cracklings are not brown yet, strain about ¼ of fat into a glass or ceramic jar so that the remaining cracklings will brown more easily.
- When all the cracklings are golden brown, strain all the remaining fat to make pork butter.
- Add milk very carefully. Heat from the fat and the new liquid can pop dangerously.
- Stir so that the milk will not burn on the bottom of the pot.
- Cook until the milk evaporates.
- By adding the milk, cracklings will become a brighter golden-brown color. They will be crunchy and very tasty.
- Let the cracklings cool, and store in the refrigerator.
- Don't save the rendered fat after milk has been added.

SERVE Pork Caviar with Czech Superstar Bread (see p. 130).

Pork Butter

Vepřové Máslo

Good homemade bread with crispy crust, smeared with homemade pork butter, topped with diced onions, and sprinkled with salt is crazy good!

4-6 SERVINGS

½ pound (250 gams) cold pork fat, saved from previous recipe

1 tablespoon (10 grams) Diamond Crystal Kosher salt

- In a bowl, whip the cold pork fat with salt until it forms peaks.

SPREAD the pork fat like you would butter over the bread. Sprinkle with finely chopped onions. Add salt to taste.

Pork Rules!

A.k.a. Praise the Lard!

Pork is an underestimated meat. The flavors of pork go much further than you think. Don't be afraid of using it. It will be better for you than some fake butters or other invented fat substitutions.

If you are lucky, someday you may cross paths with Chef Brian Polcyn, author of the book *Charcuterie*. He will probably tell you a story about a woman who loved pork fat like nothing else. She would use the beautiful white pork butter without the salt as a cream to apply on her legs. From that, her hands were silky and beautiful. Well guess who that lady was? My mother! I don't use pork fat on my body, but to each their own.

Potato Pancakes

Bramboráčky

Potato pancakes are among the treasures of Czech cuisine. Potato pancakes became widespread from the moment potatoes were first introduced in Europe, and you can find them in many world cuisines, but only Czech potato pancakes smell of garlic and marjoram. They go hand in hand with smoked meats and sauerkraut. Potato pancakes are served as a side or an appetizer and are sold on the streets.

4-6 SERVINGS

17½ ounces (500 grams) Yukon potatoes, peeled and grated

1½ cups (225-300 grams) onion, grated

2 tablespoons (18 grams) garlic, pressed

3 eggs

4 tablespoons (8 grams) dried marjoram

2 tablespoons (18 grams) garlic salt

2 teaspoons (6 grams) Diamond Crystal Kosher salt

1 teaspoon (2-2.5 grams) ground black pepper

⅔ cup plus 2 tablespoons (100 grams) all-purpose flour

1 cup (250 milliliters) vegetable oil

- Grate potatoes and onions on a coarse side of grater into a bowl. Discard the starch from potatoes and onions by squeezing it and placing the mixture into a clean bowl.
- Add garlic, eggs, marjoram, garlic salt, kosher salt, ground pepper, and flour. Mix.
- In a frying pan, heat cooking oil and scoop about 2 soup-spoons full of the mixture into it to form round pancakes.
- On medium-low heat, fry pancakes until they are golden-brown on both sides, about 15-20 minutes.
- Place pancakes on paper towel to drain, and blot the tops with another paper towel to remove excess oil.

2

Stocks

Vývary

The most important ingredient in many dishes, especially soups, is good stock. It is your ticket to success. In Czech cooking, it is "culinary gold." Use homemade stock whenever possible!

Stock is made from bones and cartilage. It contains more collagen than broth does and has a richer texture.

The recipes for stocks in this book are written to fit in 8 to 12 quart stock pots. Stock pots need to be tall rather than wide. With a smaller pot circumference, the water will evaporate more slowly than in a pot with a large opening.

Adding store-bought bouillon cubes to your stock will boost its flavor. These are available in beef, chicken, and vegetable flavors.

Beef Stock

Hovězí Vývar

Different countries call beef stock different names. The French call it *bouillon*; Spanish-speaking nations know it as *caldo*; in Italy, it's known as *brodo*. In Czechia we call it "culinary gold." When the stock is made properly, this proverb explains its strength. "A good broth will resurrect the dead!" Eat it when you get sick to speed your recovery; eat it when you're well to keep you from getting sick.

3-4 QUARTS

2 pounds (900 grams) veal bones, knuckles, and trims

3 tablespoons (40 grams) vegetable oil, or as needed

6 quarts (6 liters) cold water, reserving 1.5 quarts

1 cup (150 grams) onions, medium diced

1 cup (125 grams) carrots, medium diced

1 cup (100 grams) celery, medium diced

½ cup (50 grams) parsnips, medium diced

½ cup (50 grams) leeks, medium diced

3 bay leaves

6 whole allspice berries

8 black peppercorns

3 sprigs fresh thyme or 1 teaspoon dried thyme

- Preheat the oven to 450° F (220° C).
- Rinse the bones under cool water to remove all impurities.
- Place the bones in a pan with the oil and roast the bones for 10 minutes or until they are deep brown.
- Transfer the bones to a stock pot and fill with 4 ½ quarts cold water.
- Keep the drippings from the bones in the pan and set aside.
- To the stock pot, add bay leaves, allspice, pepper corns, and thyme. Do not stir or cover with a lid!
- Simmer over low heat for 3 hours. Skim the foam (proteins) as necessary. Do not stir or cover with a lid!
- When the liquid level drops, add reserved cold water so that the veal parts remain submerged.
- In 3 hours the liquid should be reduced by half.

- To your drippings in the roasting pan, add diced onions, celery, carrots, parsnips, and leeks, and cook about 10 minutes, or until the onions are a deep golden brown.
- For brown stock, add tomato paste and continue to cook, stirring frequently, for 2 minutes. If necessary, add a little bit of stock to the pan.
- Add the cooked vegetables to the stock and simmer for one more hour.
- Strain the stock through a fine mesh sieve (chinois), let it cool, and refrigerate.
- Discard the fat after it has solidified on top of the stock.
- If you don't use the stock immediately, store it in the refrigerator for up to 5 days or in the freezer for up to 3 months.

TIP *You can use the bones and vegetables again for a second "wash." Just add cool water and simmer for about twenty minutes. Second-wash stock will be less strong but still better than plain water.*

The veal bones, knuckles, and trims can be replaced with wild game carcass, smoked pork, lamb, or peels from vegetables (1 cup / 100 grams). Onions, carrots, parsnip, celery root are good choices for any stock.

- *For wild game add 4 juniper berries. Juniper berries are very powerful. Don't get carried away!*
- *For smoked pork add 1 teaspoon of caraway seed.*
- *For lamb add 4 juniper berries, ½ teaspoon of cumin seeds, and 1 stem of fresh rosemary.*

If using vegetables, wash them and then dice them about ½ inch wide. Grating is not suitable, as the vegetables will cook too quickly and your broth will be murky.

Chicken Stock

Kuřecí Vývar

Chicken stock is the pinnacle of culinary arts, the most flavorful stock. My favorite. You don't have to roast the bones for chicken stock because most chicken stocks should be blond. But if you would like to, you can roast them to make the stock darker. There is another trick though: if you need your chicken stock dark, add onion peel to it. It will turn your stock brown.

3-4 QUARTS

2 pounds (900 grams) chicken wings

6 quarts (6 liters) water, cold, reserving 1.5 quarts

1 cup (150 grams) onions medium diced

1 cup (125 grams) carrots, medium diced

1 cup (100 grams) celery, medium diced

½ cup (50 grams) parsnip, medium diced

½ cup (50 grams) leek, medium diced

3 bay leaves

6 whole allspice berries

8 black peppercorns

3 sprigs fresh thyme or 1 teaspoon dried thyme

- Rinse the wings under cool water to remove all impurities.
- Place the wings into a stock pot and add the cold water.
- Add bay leaves, allspice, peppercorns, and thyme.
- Simmer over low heat for 2 hours, skimming the foam as necessary. Do not stir or cover with a lid!
- As the liquid level drops, add water so that the wings remain submerged.
- Add all diced vegetables to the stock and simmer for one more hour.
- Strain the stock through a fine mesh sieve (chinois), let it cool, and refrigerate.
- Discard the fat after it has solidified on top of the stock.
- If not using immediately, store the stock in the refrigerator for up to 7 days or freeze for up to 3 months.

Left to right: Chicken, beef, and fish stock.

Fish Stock

Rybí Vývar

Eating fish once or twice a week may be beneficial. Fresh fish is available in every store, so why not to make a dish with multiple layers? Have fish stock ready for your next adventure!

3-4 QUARTS

2 pounds (900 grams) fish bones, heads, or skins

5 quarts (5 liters) water, cold, reserving 1 quart

1 cup (100 grams) celery stalk, medium diced

1 cup (100 grams) parsnip, medium diced

1 cup (100 grams) leek, medium diced

½ cup (50 grams) each of fennel, onion, mushroom, medium diced

¾ cup (175 milliliter) white wine

½ lemon, sliced

4 stems of fresh parsley

8 black peppercorns

6 whole allspice

1 sprig of fresh thyme or 1 teaspoon of dried thyme

2 bay leaves

- Rinse fish pieces under cool water.
- Fill a large pot with cold water, add fish pieces, vegetables, wine, lemon, parsley, and spices.
- Bring to a boil, then immediately reduce heat and simmer for 1 hour. Do not stir or cover with a lid!
- When the liquid level drops, add water so that the carcasses are submerged.
- Strain the stock through a fine mesh colander (chinois), allow to cool, and if not using immediately, store in the refrigerator for up to 7 days or freeze for up to 3 months.

TIP

- *If you don't have bones, heads, or skin you can use whole white fish with skin for the stock.*
- *The fish can be replaced with shrimp, lobster, or crab. Roast the crustacean shells until they are a nice golden brown.*

Ham Hock Stock

Uzený Vývar

This stock will elevate the taste of many dishes, especially soups like split pea, lentil, or any bean soup.

3-4 QUARTS

2 pounds (900 grams) smoked pork hock

6 quarts (6 liters) water, cold, reserving 1.5 quarts

3 bay leaves

6 whole allspice berries

8 black peppercorns

3 sprigs of fresh thyme or 1 teaspoon of dried thyme

1 cup (125-150 grams) each of onion, carrots, celery stalk, parsnip, medium diced

½ cup (50 grams) leeks, medium diced

- Rinse the ham hock under cool water to remove all impurities.
- Place the ham hock into a stock pot and add cold water.
- Add bay leaves, allspice, peppercorns, and thyme. Do not stir or cover with a lid!
- Simmer over low heat for 3 hours, skimming the foam as necessary.
- When the liquid level drops, add water so that the bones remain submerged.
- Add all diced vegetables to the stock and simmer for 1 more hour.
- Strain the stock through a fine mesh sieve, allow to cool, and if not using immediately, refrigerate.
- Discard the fat after it has solidified on the top of the stock.
- This stock can be stored in the freezer for 3 months.

Roux

Jíška

A roux is combination of fat and flour used for thickening soups and sauces. It is an important part of making classical sauces like Bechamel and Velouté. Prepare the roux ahead of time, because it is necessary to add cold roux to a hot liquid. It will store well in the refrigerator.

YOU WILL NEED:

3 ounces of roux per quart of liquid

4 ounces of roux per quart for medium-body sauce

5 ounces of roux per quart for thick sauce

6 ounces of roux per quart for heavy sauce

To make 1 cup of sauce, start with 2 tablespoons of fat and 2 tablespoons of flour.

Then add 1 cup of liquid.

TO MAKE 8 OUNCES (225 GRAMS)

7½ tablespoons (100 grams) unsalted butter

1 cup (125 grams) all-purpose flour

- In a saucepan, melt the butter over medium heat.
- Stir in the flour and cook for 4 minutes, stirring constantly so that the mixture will not burn. The roux should puff slightly.
- When the roux develops a golden-brown color, it is ready for use. It should resemble damp sand.
- You can store roux in the refrigerator for future use.

TIP *Some books recommend a 1:1 ratio of fat to flour. I don't find this ratio accurate, therefore I am adjusting the ratio to 1:1 ¼. This works better for me. You can always add more flour if the roux looks too wet or add more butter if the roux looks too dry.*

Add cold roux to hot liquid. Add hot roux to cold liquid. If both liquids and roux are hot the mixture will clump, and you will end up with small dumplings.

After adding roux to a liquid, the dish must be cooked for at least another 5 to 10 minutes.

The longer roux is cooked, the runnier it will become and the less thickening power it will have.

Instead of butter, you can use oil, duck fat, bacon fat, clarified butter, or any other fat.

Velouté

Veluté

This simple, stock-based sauce forms the base of all kinds of soups and many other sauces in Czech cuisine, such as horseradish or pickle sauce. Use strong beef stock for the most flavor.

4-6 SERVINGS

⅓ cup (80 grams) unsalted butter

⅔ cup plus 2 tablespoons (100 grams) all-purpose flour

1½ quarts (1½ liters) of strong stock

1 teaspoon (3 grams) Diamond Crystal Kosher salt or to taste

⅛ teaspoon (1 gram) ground white pepper

- In a saucepan, melt the butter over medium-low heat.
- Stir in flour and cook for 4 minutes. Stir frequently. The roux should puff slightly.
- Whisk in 1 cup of the stock. Stir.
- Whisk in the rest of the stock. Stir.
- Add salt and pepper.
- Simmer on medium-high for 5 minutes to reach silky consistency.
- Strain using a fine mesh sieve.

TIP *Normally the sauce will thicken when you store it in the refrigerator, so you will need to add a little liquid to it before reheating.*

You can use velouté thickener with chicken, fish, or vegetable sauces, as called for in recipes. To make velouté suprême, add 1 cup heavy cream, 1 ounce butter, salt, pepper, and lemon juice to taste to 1 quart of velouté.

Béchamel Sauce

Bešamelová Omáčka

Béchamel is a medium-thick white sauce that will add unique flavor to dill or mushroom sauce. Unlike Velouté, Béchamel is made with milk.

4-6 SERVINGS

⅓ cup (80 grams) unsalted butter

⅔ cup plus 2 tablespoons (100 grams) all-purpose flour

1½ quarts (1½ liters) milk

1 teaspoon (3 grams) Diamond Crystal Kosher salt, or to taste

⅛ teaspoon (1 gram) ground white pepper

⅛ teaspoon (1 gram) nutmeg, freshly grated

- In a saucepan, melt the butter over medium heat.
- Stir in flour and cook for 4 minutes. Stir frequently. The roux should puff slightly.
- Whisk in 1 cup of the milk. Stir.
- Whisk in the rest of the milk. Keep stirring so that the sauce at the bottom of the saucepan does not burn.
- Add salt and pepper.
- Cook for 5 minutes. Add nutmeg.
- Strain using fine mesh sieve.

TIP *Mornay Cheese Sauce: Add grated Gruyère or Emmental cheese to the sauce.*

Add this sauce to Spätzle for a fresh pasta with cheese dish.

Slurry Thickener

Záklechtka

A slurry is a mixture of flour or starch with liquid, shaken or stirred together until the flour dissolves. Slurry is an old Czech way of thickening food, especially soups.

FOR **1 QUART** OF SOUP

½ cup (125 milliliters) liquid (broth, milk, cream, or yogurt)

1 tablespoon (8 grams) all-purpose flour, arrowroot, or corn starch

- The flour, arrowroot, or corn starch can be added without lumps by floating it on top of the liquid in a jar with a leakproof lid, capping the jar tightly, and shaking vigorously for a few seconds. The liquid must always go in first. Or combine by whisking together—again floating the dry ingredients on top of the liquid before gently folding in, then whisking.
- Add slurry in small amounts to sauces and soups, stirring until well combined.
- Add more slurry if necessary to increase the thickness the sauce or soup.

TIP *Add the slurry at the end of cooking.*

3

Soups

Polévky

Czech soups are not only a first course but also a cure. The magical effect of Czech soups is widely known. Eat the soup when you are sick, eat it to keep yourself healthy, eat it to be strong . . . eat it because soups are simply great! The old Czech proverb "*Polévka je grund, kdo jí nejí bude špunt!*" says, "Soup is the foundation of our health—he who does not eat it will not grow!" Simple magic.

Dedicate one pot in your kitchen for making soups and one for making stocks. Stainless steel is the best. Cast iron skillets are also very important. Preparing food in a cast iron skillet will add traces of iron to the dish, which is especially good for women. But stay away from aluminum pots and pans. Aluminum is a very good heat conductor, but it is not good for your health. If you have an aluminum pot you absolutely love, use it, but don't scrape the bottom of it when stirring!

Czech Potato Soup

Bramboračka

The Czechs are undoubtedly a soup nation. Czech Potato Soup is called "Czech" because Czechia (the Czech Republic) is formed by three regions: Bohemia, Moravia, and Czech Silesia, and this soup comes from the Czech Silesia region. The good taste of this soup comes from a well-balanced amount of root vegetables. Don't forget to use lots of mushrooms!

6-8 SERVINGS

1½ tablespoons (20 grams) unsalted butter

1½ cups (200 grams) carrots, peeled and medium diced

¾ cup (100 grams) parsnip, peeled and medium diced

1 cup (100 grams) celery root, peeled and medium diced

¾ cup (100 grams) onions, medium diced

3 cups (250 grams) mushrooms, rinsed and sliced

1 teaspoon caraway seed, ground

3 quarts (3 liters) chicken or beef stock

4 cups (400 grams) Yukon gold potatoes, peeled and medium diced

1 tablespoon (10 grams) Diamond Crystal Kosher salt

½ teaspoon (2 grams) black ground pepper

3 tablespoons (30 grams) garlic, minced

2 tablespoons (4 grams) marjoram, dried

1 tablespoon (4 grams) parsley, chopped

½ cup (110 grams) roux

- In a large pot, sauté the carrots, parsnip, and celery root in butter over medium heat. Stir occasionally. Sweat the vegetables for about 8 minutes.
- Add onions and mushrooms, and cook a few minutes more, until onions are translucent.
- Add ground caraway seed. Stir.
- Add the stock and potatoes.
- Season with salt and pepper.
- Stir in the roux.
- Cook until potatoes are tender.
- Add garlic, marjoram, and parsley.

TIP *Crumble up dried marjoram with your fingers to open up the flavor.*

Beer Soup

Pivní Polévka

Beer is called "liquid bread" by Czechs and other nations in Europe. Beer's ability to provide nutritional value was known for centuries. In ancient times in Egypt, workers on the construction of the pyramids always got two jugs of beer in addition to bread, garlic, and onions, for their strength. Warriors and soldiers strengthened themselves before the fight with beer. In the Middle Ages, beer soups were very common.

My mother told me that good properties in beer produce good milk when breastfeeding.

Dark beer is better for the soup.

4-6 SERVINGS

4 cups (150 grams) stale bread, cubed

1 bottle (12oz) Shiner Bock dark beer

1½ tablespoons (20 grams) unsalted butter

¾ cup (100 grams) onions, sliced

1 tablespoon (7 grams) caraway seed, ground

1 tablespoon (6-8 grams) fresh ginger, finely grated

1 teaspoon lemon zest

2 tablespoons (42 grams) honey

3 cups (750 milliliters) cold water

2 egg yolks, whisked

1 pinch nutmeg

1 teaspoon (2 grams) ground white pepper

1 teaspoon (3 grams) Diamond Crystal Kosher salt

1 tablespoon (15 grams) lemon juice, freshly squeezed

- Soak the cubed bread in the beer.
- In a soup pot, heat the butter, add the onions, caraway seeds, ginger, and lemon zest, and sauté on medium-high until the onions are translucent.
- Add honey.
- Add water and bring it slowly to a simmer.
- Add soaked bread and simmer 10 minutes.

(continues)

- Add whisked egg yolks, nutmeg, pepper, and salt.
- Puree the soup with a stick (immersion) blender.
- Add squeezed lemon juice.

SERVE with fresh homemade croutons.

Bohemian Cabbage Soup

Zelná Polévka s Uzeninkou

Evidence of this soup's popularity is confirmed in the saying, "Cabbage soup for breakfast, cabbage soup for dinner." The roasted kielbasa makes this a great hearty soup. Use jalapeno kielbasa to add a spicy kick.

4-6 SERVINGS

¼ cup (50 grams) bacon, small diced

2 tablespoons (28 grams) vegetable oil

9 ounces (250 grams) kielbasa sausage, medium diced

¾ cup (100 grams) onions, medium diced

3 quarts (3 liters) beef stock

2 cups (300 grams) Yukon gold potatoes, medium diced

2 teaspoons (6 grams) Diamond Crystal Kosher salt

½ teaspoon (1.5 grams) black ground pepper

⅓ cup (60 grams) roux

3½ cups (300 grams) fresh white cabbage, large diced

2 tablespoons (30 grams) white vinegar

2 tablespoons (4 grams) marjoram

1 tablespoon (9 grams) garlic, minced

1 tablespoon (4 grams) parsley, chopped

- In a soup pot, render the bacon over low heat, 6–8 minutes.
- Add diced kielbasas and roast in the pan until fragrant, to open up the flavor.
- Add onions and sweat them together with kielbasas about 4 minutes, or until the onions are translucent.
- Add stock, potatoes, salt, and pepper. Bring the soup slowly to a boil.
- Turn the heat down immediately and simmer for 20 minutes, stirring occasionally, until the potatoes are tender.
- Stir in the roux.
- Add white cabbage, vinegar, marjoram, and pressed garlic. Cook for an additional 8–10 minutes.

SERVE with sprinkled chopped parsley.

Cream of Cauliflower Soup

Květáková Polévka

People have been enjoying cauliflower for a long time. Cauliflower can be boiled, baked, stewed, roasted, or fried. There are no limits to the imagination when preparing cauliflower. Raw cauliflower is crispy and has a slightly sharper taste. When cooked properly, cauliflower has a sweet to nutty taste. A typical Czech dish at almost all restaurants is fried cauliflower with potatoes and tartar sauce.

4-6 SERVINGS

1½ tablespoons (20 grams) unsalted butter

½ cup (50 grams) onions, medium diced

3 quarts (3 liters) chicken stock

5½ cups (500 grams) cauliflower, cut into small pieces

2 cups (300 grams) potatoes, medium diced

1½ cups (150 grams) white part of leek, sliced

1 tablespoon (10 grams) Diamond Crystal Kosher salt

½ teaspoon (1.5 grams) white ground pepper

Pinch of nutmeg

½ cup (100 milliliters) heavy cream

2 tablespoons (15 grams) all-purpose flour

3 tablespoons (9 grams) chives, chopped

- In a soup pot, heat the butter, add the onions, and cook on medium-high 5–8 minutes, or until the onions are translucent.
- Add chicken stock, cauliflower, diced potatoes, and leek. Set aside a few florets of cauliflower to use later. Bring the soup slowly to a boil, and immediately reduce the heat. Continue to simmer until the potatoes are tender.
- Add salt, pepper, and nutmeg.
- Puree the soup in a blender with heavy cream and flour.
- Pour the soup back into the pot, and bring it gently to a simmer for 5 minutes. Do not boil.

SERVE with cauliflower florets and sprinkle with chopped chives.

TIP *Add a couple of pats of butter on top of the soup to prevent it from forming a skin.*

History of Asparagus

It was not until the beginning of the 19th century that the most famous asparagus plantations were established in the Czech Republic's southern Moravian town Ivancice (home of the artist Alfons Mucha).

The complexity of cultivating asparagus from seed to the actual vegetable is difficult, so the price tag for asparagus meant that it could only be enjoyed by "high society." So when the Communist Party took over the Czech lands in 1948, production of asparagus stopped because kohlrabi and cabbage were supposed to be good enough for the average person.

Today other countries in the Europe are producing asparagus, but they push the growth 300% higher than it should be. They don't let the soil rest, and therefore the quality of the asparagus is not the same as the asparagus from Ivancice. As the proverb says: "Less is more!"

A soil expert who evaluated the soil of Ivancice, discovered earthworms and enthusiastically explained that earthworms no longer occur in commercial soils squeezed to the maximum. If they are there, it means that the soil is "tasty," so it is rich and healthy!

White Czech asparagus is a particular delicacy of the Czech gastronomy.

The name of "asparagus" came from the Persian *sparega*. The Greeks named it *asparagos*, and the name of the vegetable in most languages is derived from this word, as you can see below.

German – *Spargel*

Polish – *Szparag*

Serb – Croatian – *Sparog*

Russian – *Sparza*

Hungarian – *Sparge*

Romanian – *Sparanghel*

Dutch – *Aspergie*

Swedish – *Asypparagasy*

Korean – *Esparago*

English – *Asparagus*

But it is only the Czechs who call asparagus something totally different: *chřest*. *Chřest* comes from the word "rattlesnake" (*chřestýš*) because the tips of asparagus look like the tails of rattlesnakes.

Cream of Asparagus Soup

Chřestová Polévka

Local Czech asparagus gained a reputation as the best all over Europe. It was better known than even beer.

4-6 SERVINGS

3 quarts (3 liters) water

2 pounds (900 grams) asparagus

1 bay leaf

6 whole allspice berries

1 sprig fresh thyme or ½ teaspoon dried thyme

1¾ cups (250 grams) Idaho potatoes, peeled, medium diced

1 tablespoon (10 grams) Diamond Crystal Kosher salt (Start with about half this amount if using another brand and adjust to taste.)

½ teaspoon (1.5 grams) white ground pepper

½ cup (125 milliliters) half-and-half

2 tablespoons (15 grams) all-purpose flour

¼ cup (60 milliliters) heavy cream

- Trim the woody ends off asparagus.
- In a stock pot, bring water to a boil and add woody asparagus stems, bay leaf, allspice, and thyme. Cook for 30 minutes.
- Strain the broth, discard ends, and return broth to the pot.
- Add potatoes and trimmed green asparagus spears to the broth (save a few tips for garnish).
- Season with salt and white pepper, and let simmer for 20–30 minutes, or until the potatoes are tender.
- Blanch saved asparagus tips in boiling water for 3 minutes, drain, and put on ice.
- In a clean container make a slurry from half-and-half and flour.
- Add the slurry to the soup, and cook for an additional 10 minutes.
- Puree the soup in a blender, and pass the mixture through a fine mesh sieve back into the pot.
- Bring the soup to a simmer over medium-high heat.
- Stir in heavy cream. Adjust the seasoning.

GARNISH the soup with blanched asparagus tips.

Chicken Broth with Semolina Gnocchi

Kuřecí Vývar s Krupicovými Noky

A flavorful soup rich with vitamins and minerals. It is useful against colds. Semolina gnocchi instead of pasta makes this soup special.

4-6 SERVINGS

3 quarts (3 liters) water

2 bay leaves

6 whole allspice berries, dried

8 black peppercorns

Pinch of dry thyme

6 chicken thighs with skin, rinsed

1 tablespoon (10 grams) Diamond Crystal Kosher salt (start with about half this amount if using another brand and adjust to taste)

1 cup (100 grams) carrots, medium diced

½ cup (50 grams) parsnip, medium diced

½ cup (50 grams) celery root, medium diced

1/2 cup (100 grams) onions, medium diced

1 tablespoon (4 grams) parsley, chopped

Semolina Gnocchi (see recipe on p. 66)

- Fill soup pot with water, bay leaves, allspice, peppercorns, and thyme.
- Add chicken thighs. Bring to a boil, then immediately reduce heat and simmer until meat falls from the bone, about 90 minutes. Do not stir.
- Add salt.
- Take the chicken thighs out, let them cool, and peel the meat from the bone.
- Strain the broth.
- Add diced carrots, parsnip, and celery root to broth.
- Cook until the vegetables are tender, about 10 minutes.
- Add the chicken meat and gnocchi and heat to serving temperature.
- Sprinkle chopped chives on top.

Cream of Leek Soup with Potatoes

Porková Polévka

You don't need too many ingredients to make this soup. Czechs eat this soup warm, but you can also serve it cold. Cold leek soup with potatoes in France is called *Vichyssoise*. As the story goes, Louis XV was afraid of being poisoned and had so many servants to taste the soup that by the time he could eat it the soup was cold. He enjoyed it very much, and voila we have a recipe for two soups in one.

4-6 SERVINGS

1½ tablespoons (20 grams) unsalted butter

¼ cup (50 grams) onions, finely chopped

2 tablespoons (15 grams) all-purpose flour

2 quarts (2 liters) chicken stock

2¼ cups (350 grams) Idaho potatoes, medium diced

4 cups (300 grams) leeks, finely sliced, white part preferably

1 tablespoon (10 grams) Diamond Crystal Kosher salt (If using another brand, start with about half this amount and adjust to taste.)

½ teaspoon (1.5 grams) white ground pepper

Pinch of nutmeg

1 cup (200 milliliters) heavy cream

1 tablespoon (4 grams) chives, finely chopped

Spice reduction:

1 cup (250 milliliters) cold water

2 stems parsley

½ teaspoon (2 grams) dried thyme

1 bay leaf

1 clove garlic

- Simmer all ingredients for spice reduction in water. Reduce to half. Strain. Reserve for soup.
- In a soup pot, heat the butter, add the onions, and sauté them over medium-high heat for 5–8 minutes, or until they are translucent.
- Add flour. Stir.
- Add stock, spice reduction, diced potatoes, leeks, salt, and pepper.
- Simmer until the potatoes are tender, about 20 minutes.
- Add nutmeg. Puree the soup in a blender, adding the heavy cream near the end of the process.
- Adjust salt to taste.

SERVE hot or cold. Sprinkle chives on top before serving.

Cream of Mushroom

Krémová Houbová Polévka

Mushroom hunting is one of the most widespread Czech traditions. Czechs are considered to be the most passionate mushrooms pickers in the world!

4-6 SERVINGS

1½ tablespoons (20 grams) unsalted butter

½ cup (50 grams) onions, sliced

1 tablespoon (7 grams) caraway seed, ground

1 pound (450 grams) mushrooms, rinsed and sliced

2 quarts (2 liters) chicken stock

2 cups (300 grams) Idaho potatoes, medium diced

½ cup (100 milliliters) heavy cream

1 tablespoon (10 grams) Diamond Crystal Kosher salt (If using another brand, start with half this amount and adjust to taste)

½ teaspoon (1.5 grams) white ground pepper

Pinch of nutmeg

- In a soup pot, heat the butter, add the onions, and sauté over medium-high heat for 5–8 minutes, or until onions are translucent.
- Add caraway seeds. Stir.
- Add rinsed mushrooms and cover for five minutes so that the mushrooms will release their juices (save a few slices of cooked mushroom for garnish).
- Add stock, potatoes, salt, pepper, and nutmeg. Bring the soup to a boil and immediately reduce heat. Simmer until the potatoes are tender, about 20 minutes.
- Puree the soup in a blender with heavy cream.
- Pour the soup back into the pot, and gently simmer for 5 minutes. Do not boil.
- Adjust the seasoning.

SERVE with a large roasted slice of mushroom on the top.

Free Forest and Alley Food in Czechia

The forest gives ample free food.

Mushroom hunting is one of the most widespread Czech traditions. Czechs are considered to be the most passionate mushroom pickers in the world! At least once a year over 70 percent of the population of the Czech Republic goes mushroom hunting.

There is no Czech summer without blueberries. These small, deep-blue berries are among the most popular fruits of the forest, right after the mushrooms. In Czech lands you are not likely to find blueberries for sale in stores. Plan your weekend around the blueberry hunt; go to the forest and pick your own. There may be limits on how many of them you can pick, but you can certainly pick as many as you can eat on the spot!

The picturesque tree alleys in the Czech Republic were planted by our ancestors over one hundred years ago. Long wars led the government to order the planting of fruit trees (apple, pear, sugar plum, and cherry) along the sides of the roads. When soldiers were coming back from far lands and were tired and hungry, they would have something to eat. These trees survived many years and you could always pick their fruit if you were hungry. I used to climb a cherry tree and eat so many cherries that my stomach bulged.

Cream of Sauerkraut

Zelnačka

This traditional soup has a number of variants, which confirms the important role of this healthy soup for winter days. It is creamy, a little sweet, a little sour, and very healthy.

4-6 SERVINGS

1½ cups (150 grams) onions, sliced

3 tablespoons (40 grams) vegetable oil

1 tablespoon (7 grams) whole caraway seeds

3 quarts (3 liters) chicken stock

2½ cups (400 grams) Idaho potatoes, medium diced

3 cups (450 grams) sauerkraut, lightly rinsed

1 tablespoon (10 grams) Diamond Crystal Kosher salt (If using another brand, start with half this amount and adjust to taste.)

3 tablespoons (42 grams) vinegar

3 tablespoons (40 grams) unsalted butter

SLURRY

1 cup (250 milliliters) half-and-half

2 tablespoons (15 grams) all-purpose flour

- In a soup pot, sauté the onions in vegetable oil with caraway seeds until the onions are translucent.
- Add stock, potatoes, and salt.
- Bring to a boil, then immediately reduce heat to medium-high.
- Simmer until the potatoes are tender, about 20 minutes.
- Add sauerkraut and slurry.
- Simmer for an additional 15 minutes, or until the soup thickens.
- Season with salt and vinegar.
- Add butter.

TIP *When you are rinsing the sauerkraut from a can or glass jar, first taste it. Is it very sour or mild? Depending on how sour the kraut is, run it under cold water to rinse it. Sauerkraut from a can is much stronger tasting than sauerkraut from a glass jar, which is usually more mellow and needs less rinsing. Do not overrinse or you will lose the kraut's specific taste.*

Moravian Cabbage Soup

Moravská Zelnačka

Moravian Cabbage Soup is historically eaten for breakfast. This soup ensured that the men of the village had enough strength to work in the forest. It is said that one plate is so filling that there is no room for lunch. In other words, serve this as a meal and you will not run out of energy.

4-6 SERVINGS

½ cup (60 grams) bacon, small diced

2 tablespoons (27 grams) vegetable oil

1 cup (100 grams) onions, sliced

12 ounces (340 grams) smoked kielbasa sausage, medium diced

3 tablespoons (20 grams) Hungarian paprika

2 teaspoons (5 grams) ground cumin

⅓ cup (40 grams) all-purpose flour

3 quarts (3 liters) ham hock stock

2½ cups (400 grams) Idaho potatoes, medium diced

1 pound (450 grams) sauerkraut, lightly rinsed

1 tablespoon (9 grams) minced garlic

1 tablespoon (10 grams) Diamond Crystal Kosher salt (If using another brand, start with half this amount and adjust to taste.)

2 tablespoons (4 grams) cilantro, chopped

2 tablespoons (8 grams) parsley, chopped

6 tablespoons (100 grams) sour cream, for garnish

Pinch of pepper, or to taste

- In a soup pot, render bacon with oil over low heat 4–6 minutes.
- Add sliced onions and diced kielbasas, and sweat until the onions are translucent.
- Add Hungarian paprika and ground cumin. Stir so that paprika will release its flavor and color.
- Sprinkle the flour and stir again. (You just made a paprika roux).
- Add the stock, use the whisk, and incorporate paprika roux into the stock.
- Add diced potatoes and sauerkraut, and cook until the potatoes are tender. About 20 minutes.
- Add garlic, salt, cilantro, parsley, and adjust with salt and pepper to taste.

SERVE with a dob of sour cream and sprinkled parsley.

TIP *For a spicier flavor, replace one smoked kielbasa sausage with 3 oz. (85 grams) of smoked jalapeno kielbasa, medium diced.*

Czech Onion Soup

Cibulačka

The oldest collections of Czech folk songs and dances come from the early 19th century. They are known as Rittersberk's Collection of Folkloric Songs under the German title *Bohmische Volkslieder – České Národní Písně.*

In 1820, there were 100,000 registered songs in the "Governor's Collection" (*Guberniální sběr*). The song about onions became one of my favorites.

Hop hej cibulá-a-ři, cibulá-a-ři jé-e-dou!
Hop hej cibuli-i-čku, cibuli-i-čku véezou!
Hop-Hey onion man, the onion man is coming!
Hop-hey bringing us onions, onions!

4-6 SERVINGS

3½ tablespoons (50 grams) unsalted butter

2 tablespoons (28 grams) vegetable oil

2½ cups (250 grams) yellow onions, sliced

½ cup (100 milliliters) red wine

1 tablespoon (7 grams) caraway seed, ground

1 tablespoon (12 grams) sugar

1 tablespoon (10 grams) Diamond Crystal Kosher salt (If using another brand, start with half this amount and adjust to taste.)

½ teaspoon (1.5 grams) black ground pepper

2½ quarts (2.5 liters) beef stock

1 bay leaf

½ teaspoon (1.5 grams) dried thyme

- Heat butter and oil in a large soup pot. Add onions.
- Cook the onions over medium-high heat for about 30 minutes, stirring occasionally until the onions are golden brown. If all the liquid evaporates before the onions are golden brown and the onions stick to the bottom of the pot, add a little beef stock. Keep stirring.
- Add red wine, and reduce it until it reaches a syrupy consistency.
- Add ground caraway seeds, sugar, salt, and pepper. Stir.
- Add beef stock, bay leaf, and thyme. Simmer the soup for about 20 minutes.
- Adjust the salt and pepper to taste.

SERVE with homemade croutons (see p. 71).

TIP *Make sure to simmer the onions on low heat. This will bring out the sugars from the onions and give the soup a stronger and more robust taste!*

If parts of the onion get too dark, you can pull them out easily after you add the stock. They will float on the top of the stock.

History of Onion Soup

According to Public Vergilius Maro (70–19 BC), Romans found Czech lands to be the most desirable territory for expanding their so-called Roman Vegetable Gardens.

One of the oldest finds ever in Europe was the discovery of well-preserved garlic plants (bulbs) in Eneolithic containers at Kyjov, Moravia (5000–4000BC). Onions and garlic were sustainable supplies for cooking in every country home in this area. Making onion soup originated here.

So why is French Onion Soup is called French?

The Battle of Austerlitz (Bitva u Slavkova) in 1805, also known as the Battle of Three Emperors, was the only a battle in history where three emperors met. It was here that Napoleon achieved his greatest victory by defeating the other two emperors.

Allegedly, the day before the battle, the Austrian and Russian emperors spent the night in the Château of Slavkov, which was not big enough to host all three emperors; therefore Napoleon had to stay elsewhere. He was upset because the château had made a big impression on him. So after his victory he expelled the two rival emperors from the château.

He celebrated his victory with the best wines and food from this region. Onion soup was one of the courses. He brought the idea to his own court in France, and the French added toast with cheese on top of soup. That is why, today, onion soup is called French Onion Soup.

Garlic Soup *or* Cure Soup

Česnečka

This is the magic soup which makes a person who is sick feel better. That's why it is called Cure Soup. I make this soup for my family when they are coming down with a cold. Try it—it really works.

4-6 SERVINGS

1½ quarts (1.5 liters) chicken or beef stock

2½ cups (350 grams) red potatoes with skin on, washed and medium diced

2 tablespoons (18 grams) garlic, pressed

1 tablespoon (4 grams) parsley, chopped

Diamond Crystal Kosher salt to taste

- In a soup pot with stock, add potatoes. Bring to a boil, then immediately reduce the heat and simmer until potatoes are tender, about 10 minutes.
- Add minced garlic, parsley, and salt to taste.
- Remove from heat.

SERVE with homemade croutons (see p. 71).

Fish Soup

Rybí Polévka

Fish Soup is always part of a traditional Czech Christmas dinner. This course is followed by Breaded Fillet of Carp with Czech Potato Salad. Dessert consists of an assortment of Czech Christmas cookies.

4-6 SERVINGS

3½ tablespoons (50 grams) unsalted butter

1½ cups (200 grams) carrots, small diced

¾ cup (100 grams) parsnip, small diced

⅓ cup (50 grams) celery root, small diced

5 cloves garlic

3 quarts (3 liters) fish stock

3½ tablespoons (50 grams) unsalted butter for roux

⅓ cup (50 grams) all-purpose flour for roux

Diamond Crystal Kosher salt to taste

Black ground pepper to taste

½ cup (50 grams) leeks, sliced

¾ pound (350 grams) fish, skinless, cut into 1½ inch pieces (filets of catfish, walleye, or of course carp)

2 tablespoons (8 grams) parsley, chopped

- In a sauté pan, sweat diced carrots, parsnip, celery root, and garlic in butter over medium heat for about 4–6 minutes. Add a pinch of salt. Stir and set aside.
- In a soup pot, melt butter and add flour. Stir to make a roux. Add 2 cups of cold fish stock and continuously stir. Add the rest of stock and cook for about 10–15 minutes.
- Add leek, pieces of fish, and prepared vegetables. Season it with salt and pepper.
- Simmer until the fish is cooked, 6–8 minutes.

SERVE with homemade croutons on top or, as we did in our picture, with Sponge Cake Garnish (see recipe p. 68). Sprinkle with fresh chopped parsley.

Lentil Soup

Čočková Polévka

On New Year's Eve, Czechs eat lentils for good luck. The lentils, with their coin-like shape, represent wealth and prosperity for the whole year.

4-6 SERVINGS

1 pound (450 grams) brown lentils

1½ tablespoons (20 grams) unsalted butter

¾ cup (100 grams) onions, diced

½ cup (60 grams) celery stalks, small diced

½ cup (60 grams) carrots, small diced

½ cup (100 grams) tomatoes, small diced

2 quarts (2 liters) beef or ham hock stock

1 tablespoon (10 grams) Diamond Crystal Kosher salt (if using another brand, start with about half this amount and adjust to taste).

Pinch of black pepper

1 tablespoon (9 grams) garlic, minced

2 cups water

2 tablespoons (8 grams) parsley, chopped

2 tablespoons (8 grams) cilantro, chopped

3 tablespoons (42 grams) vinegar

- Soak lentils in a bowl of cold water for 10 minutes. Rinse.
- In a soup pan, sauté onions, celery stalk, carrots, and tomatoes in butter until tender.
- Add drained lentils and then stock so that the stock covers the vegetables and lentils by about 2 inches.
- Add salt and pepper.
- Simmer until lentils are tender, about 15–20 minutes.
- Add garlic.
- In the blender, puree ¼ of the soup until it is smooth (this will thicken the soup).
- Add the pureed mixture back to the soup.
- Rinse the blender with 1–2 cups of water and add to the soup.
- Add chopped parsley and cilantro.
- Add vinegar to taste.

History of the Word "Dollar"

Since we are talking about the lentils and their shape that resembles a coin, have you ever wondered where the word "dollar" came from?

Ironic fact: The US dollar is the most widely used currency in the world. Sixty-two percent of the planet's financial reserves are held in US dollars. Yet one place where the dollar is not accepted is in the tiny Czech town of Jachymov, the place where the dollar originated 500 years ago.

On January 15, 1520, the Kingdom of Bohemia began minting coins from silver in Joachimosthal and marked the reverse with the Bohemian two-tailed lion. Since the silver for these coins was found in Saint Joachim's Valley in Bohemia, the coins became known as *Joachimsthalers*. Over time, this was shortened to *thaler*. Countries across Europe began renaming their coins after the thaler in their own languages.

In Denmark, Norway, and Sweden, the thaler became known as the *daalder*. In Iceland it was *dalur*. In Italy *tallero*. In Poland *talar*. In Greece *taliro*. In Hungary *taller*. In France the derivation of *thaler* is *Jocandale* (coming from the town Jachymov). In Slovenia *tolar*.

The thaler spread to Africa, across the Arab Peninsula, into India and as far as Singapore, Fiji, and Australia. The currency in Romania is *leu*, in Bulgaria *lev*, in Moldovia *leu*—all derived from the lion stamped on the first thaler 500 years ago.

Thanks to trade with the Dutch and the English, the Dutch *leeuwendaler*, "lion dollar," or *daler* for short, was brought to North America in the 17th century with Dutch colonists, and the usage spread quickly through the Thirteen Colonies. The settlers began to call all similarly weighted silver coins, including the widely used Spanish *real de a ocho* (piece-of-eight) coin "dollars."

Split Pea Soup

Hrášková Polévka

Pea soup has been part of the classic folk cuisine for centuries. It was widely cooked in country cottages as "food for the poor." It was filling, inexpensive, and nutritious.

In contrast, in this century the soup is found on the menus of luxury restaurants, and in many families it is the second most common choice for the Christmas Eve menu after fish soup.

4-6 SERVINGS

1 pound (450 grams) split peas

6 ounces (170 grams) kielbasa sausage, medium diced

2 tablespoons (28 grams) vegetable oil

3 quarts (3 liters) ham hock stock

1¼ cups (200 grams) Idaho potatoes, peeled, small diced

1 tablespoon (9 grams) garlic, minced

Diamond Crystal Kosher salt to taste

1 teaspoon (2-2.5 grams) black ground pepper

- Soak split peas in a bowl of cold water for 30 minutes. Rinse.
- In a soup pot, sauté diced kielbasa in the oil over medium-high heat.
- Remove the sausage and set aside.
- Deglaze the drippings on the bottom of the pot with 1 cup of stock.
- Add the rest of the stock, drained split peas, and diced potatoes.
- Simmer until split peas are tender. Stir occasionally. Cook for about 20–30 minutes.
- Add garlic, salt, and pepper.
- Puree the soup in a blender until it is smooth.
- Pour the soup back into the pot and gently simmer for 5 minutes. Do not boil.
- Adjust the seasonings.
- Add the roasted sausages.

SERVE with homemade croutons.

Does this story make us peas in a pod?

Mendel's Law: Pea plants are connected to the discovery of genetics and the three laws of inheritance. Czech born Gregor Johann Mendel (1822-1884) was born in Heizendorf (now Hynčice, Czech Republic). Through his work on pea plants, he deduced that genes come in pairs and are inherited as distinct units, one from each parent.

Tomato Soup

Rajská Polévka

Czech tomato soup is very different from Italian tomato soup. It does not include garlic, bell peppers, or oregano. It is a pure paradise of cinnamon, cloves, lemon peel, and good beef stock.

4-6 SERVINGS

3 tablespoons (40 grams) unsalted butter

½ cup (50 grams) onions, diced

10 black peppercorns

6 whole allspice berries

1 teaspoon (2 grams) cinnamon

2 bay leaves

1 sprig fresh thyme or 1 teaspoon dried thyme

7 whole cloves

Peel of half a lemon, cut into strips

¼ cup (50 grams) sugar

⅓ cup (40 grams) all-purpose flour

1 pound 12 ounces (794 grams) canned whole peeled tomatoes

6 ounces (170 grams) tomato paste

3 quarts (3 liters) beef stock

1 tablespoon (10 grams) Diamond Crystal Kosher salt (If using another brand, start with about half this amount and adjust to taste.)

- In a soup pot, sauté onions, peppercorns, allspice, cinnamon, bay leaves, thyme, clove, and lemon peel in butter until the onions are translucent.
- Add sugar. Stir.
- Add flour. Stir.
- Add the whole peeled tomatoes and tomato paste. Simmer and stir for 3 minutes.
- Add beef stock and bring slowly to a boil, then immediately reduce heat and simmer for 20 minutes.
- Season with salt.
- Add more sugar if needed.
- Remove bay leaf, peppercorns, allspice, and lemon peel.
- Puree the soup in a blender.
- Pour the soup back into the pot and simmer for an additional 5 minutes.

SERVE with homemade croutons.

TIP *As an alternative to using canned whole tomatoes, you can freeze 2 pounds of fresh tomatoes. Peel the skin off when they are semi-frozen, and diced.*

Kulayda with a Poached Egg

Kulajda

This soup was created by mushroom lovers, and it is prepared all over the country, from the Bohemian Forest (Šumava) to the Giant Mountains (Krkonoše) throughout central Moravia to the Jeseníky Mountains. Every family has its own recipe, and I would like to share mine.

This is a sweet-and-sour cream soup with fresh mushrooms, dill, and diced potatoes. The soup is thickened with a butter/flour paste called Beurre Manie.

4-6 SERVINGS

3 quarts (3 liters) water

3.5 oz (100 grams) bouquet of fresh dill

2 tablespoons (30 grams) unsalted butter

4 cups (250 grams) mushrooms, sliced

2½ cups (400 grams) Idaho potatoes, medium diced

1 cup (250 grams) heavy cream

2 teaspoons (6 grams) Diamond Crystal Kosher salt (if using another brand, start with about half this amount and adjust to taste).

½ teaspoon (1.5 grams) white ground pepper to taste

⅓ cup (70 grams) sugar

⅓ cup distilled white vinegar, or to taste

1 egg per person

BEURRE MANIE

¼ cup (60 grams) unsalted butter

⅓ cup plus 1 tablespoon (50 grams) all-purpose flour

- In a pot, simmer dill stems in water for 1 hour. Discard the stems, keep the dill broth.
- In a small pan, sauté sliced mushrooms in butter until they are golden brown. Put them to the side for later use.
- In a soup pot make a Beurre Manie: Warm up the butter and add the flour. Stir.
- When the Beurre Manie develops a paste consistency, add 1 cup of dill broth. Stir.
- Add rest of the dill broth, diced potatoes, salt, white pepper, and sautéed mushrooms.
- Cook the soup on medium-high until the potatoes are tender. About 20 minutes.
- Add sugar and vinegar. Stir.
- Add heavy cream, and simmer for a few minutes.
- Take it off the burner, and add the fresh chopped dill.

POACHED EGG

- In a small pot, bring water to simmer.
- Add 1 tablespoon of vinegar and an egg. Stir so that the egg will not stick to the bottom of the pot.
- Simmer until the egg white is fully cooked and yolk is still runny, about 4 minutes.
- Remove the egg with a slotted spoon and place it on an absorbent towel to dry.

TO SERVE: Ladle the soup in the soup bowl, and place the poached egg in the middle. Sprinkle with fresh chopped dill.

Holiday Soup with Liver Dumplings

Polévka s Játrovými Knedličky

You can prepare this soup at any time. You don't have wait until Christmas. The reason it used to be made only on holidays is because liver was not available all the time and was more expensive, so this soup was reserved for special days.

4-6 SERVINGS

3 quarts (3 liters) beef stock

2 pounds (900 grams) chicken thighs

1 cube of chicken bouillon

Liver Dumplings (in my family we like at least 5 liver dumplings per person)

2 tablespoons (8 ounces) parsley, chopped

1 tablespoon (9 grams) garlic, minced

Diamond Crystal Kosher salt to taste

- First make Liver Dumplings (p.70) and refrigerate.
- Add chicken thighs and chicken bouillon to prepared beef stock and cook for one hour. Additional cooking time makes the flavor deeper.
- Strain the stock.
- Add liver dumplings and cook them for 3–5 minutes or until they come up to the surface.
- Add garlic and parsley.

Tripe Soup

Dršťková Polévka

In Czechia, tripe soup is known as the "soup of railway restaurants." It is a hearty breakfast, a tasty snack, and a quick dinner. It is known for being a cure for hangovers! In my recipe I am adding carrots and celery to elevate the flavor.

4-6 SERVINGS

½ cup (68 grams) Diamond Crystal Kosher salt for rubbing

1½ pounds (680 grams) honeycomb tripe, soaked overnight in water

6 quarts (6 liters) water for cooking tripe

1 cup (240 milliliters) vinegar

¾ cup (100 grams) each of onions, carrot, and celery stalk, medium diced

⅓ cup (76 grams) pork fat

3 tablespoons (20 grams) Hungarian paprika

4 tablespoons (30 grams) all-purpose flour

1 quart (1 liter) tripe stock

1½ quarts (1.5 liters) beef stock

2¼ cups (350 grams) Idaho potatoes, peeled, medium diced

2 tablespoons (30 grams) garlic, pressed

1 tablespoon (2 grams) dried marjoram

1 tablespoon (10 grams) Diamond Crystal Kosher salt (if using another brand, start with about half this amount and adjust to taste).

Pepper to taste

1 tablespoon (4 grams) parsley, chopped

DIRECTIONS FOR THE TRIPE STOCK:

- Rub the soaked tripe with salt and then scrape the salt off with a knife to remove impurities. Rinse the tripe and brush again with a clean toothbrush.
- Place washed tripe in cold water with vinegar and bring to a boil, then immediately reduce heat and simmer for 30 minutes.
- Discard the water and fill the pot with fresh cold water. Repeat the second step.
- Place the tripe in a stock pot and add fresh cold water once again. Bring to a boil, then immediately reduce heat and simmer for 3 hours or until tripe is tender. Do not stir or cover with a lid. If you wish to use a pressure cooker at this point, cook for 30–45 minutes, starting the time right after you hear the first whistle from the pressure cooker.
- If the liquid reduces too much and the tripe is not tender yet, add more water so that the tripe is submerged.
- Strain the stock through a fine mesh colander into new pot and set aside.
- Cut the tripe into small strips.

DIRECTIONS FOR SOUP:

- In a clean soup pot, sauté onions in the pork fat for 4–6 minutes. Add the diced carrot and celery and sauté for an additional 4 minutes.
- Add the paprika, stir, and then add the flour. Stir. You just created paprika roux with carrots and celery.
- In a separate container mix 1 quart (1 liter) of tripe stock with 1½ quarts (1.5 liters) beef stock.
- Slowly add part of the mixed stocks. Whisk so that the paprika roux melts into the soup.
- Add the rest of mixed stocks to the pot.
- Add potatoes and tripe. Simmer for 20 minutes, or until potatoes are tender.
- Add garlic and marjoram, and adjust seasoning with salt and pepper.

TIP *If you have a pressure cooker, it will shorten the cooking time, capture all the flavors, and make the stock stronger.*

4

Soup Garnishes and Fillers

Vložky do Polévek

We know that most of the soups are thickened with a roux or slurry. But the Czech proverb says, "It's not soup, like soup" (*Není polévka, jako polévka*) until you finish it with some kind of filler. Soup garnishes and fillers not only thicken the soup, but also increase its nutritional value.

There are abundant recipes for different fillers, garnishes, drippings, gnocchis, and dumplings in Czech cuisine. Czech grandmothers carry an arsenal of soup supplements. Traditional Czech cuisine knows so many of them that the soup garnish or filler does not need to be repeated twice in a month. They can be made out of flour, potatoes, bread, meat, liver, marrow, ham, mushrooms, eggs, noodles, and even yeast.

There are two general ways to make a soup more filling.

"Garnishes" are cooked outside of the soup and then added to the soup just before serving. You must make sure that these fillers are hot before adding them to the soup. Some examples of garnishes are poached eggs, celestine noodles, gnocchi, and croutons.

Fillers are cooked directly in the soup. An example of a filler is liver dumplings.

Semolina Gnocchi

Krupicové Noky do Polévky

The texture of gnocchi is firm to the bite but melts in your mouth.

4-6 SERVINGS

2 tablespoons plus 2 teaspoons (30 grams) softened unsalted butter

1 large egg

¾ cup (150 milliliters) milk

1 teaspoon (3 grams) Diamond Crystal Kosher salt (if using another brand, start with about half this amount and adjust to taste).

1¼ cups (200 grams) semolina flour

1 tablespoon (4 grams) parsley, chopped

6 quarts (6 liters) water

1 tablespoon (10 grams) Diamond Crystal Kosher salt, for boiling water (see above)

Butter for smearing gnocchi

- In a mixing bowl, whisk butter with an egg.
- Add milk and 1 teaspoon salt. Whisk.
- Add flour. With a wooden spoon, incorporate flour with the liquid into a smooth dough. If the dough is too runny, add more flour.
- Add parsley.
- Let rest for 15 minutes in refrigerator.
- In a separate pot, bring 6 quarts salted water to boil.
- With a spoon, create small gnocchi and place into boiling water.
- Reduce the heat to medium.
- Cook the gnocchi for about 6 minutes, or until they float to the top. The time depends on the size of your gnocchi. Adjust the time by pulling one out of the pot after it rises to the top and cutting it open in the middle to see if the dough is cooked thoroughly.
- Remove cooked gnocchi from the water and coat with melted butter so that they will not dry out.

Celestine Noodles

Celestýnské Nudle

These noodles are named after a young girl named Celestine, who was a mistress of chef from Lyon, France. He created this recipe and named it after her. Celestine noodles are thin crepes cut into strips 2–2.5 inches long and ½ inch wide. They are placed in the broth soup when serving. In summer add fresh herbs, garlic, chives, celery stalk, or lovage instead of parsley. You can use whole grain instead of all-purpose flour.

4-6 SERVINGS

½ cup plus 1 tablespoon (160 milliliter) milk

1 egg

½ cup plus 2 teaspoons (75 grams) all-purpose flour

Pinch of Diamond Crystal Kosher salt or to taste

2 tablespoons (8 grams) parsley, chopped

Butter for making the crepes

- In a blender, mix milk, egg, flour, and salt on high speed.
- Pour the batter into a mixing bowl and add parsley. Stir.
- Let it rest in the refrigerator for half an hour. If the batter separates, mix it with a fork before making the crepes.
- In a pan with butter, pour a small ladle of batter to form thin crepes. Cook for 3 minutes on each side.
- Roll the crepes and slice into noodles about ½ in. wide.

Sponge Cake Garnish

Piškotový Svítek

Sponge Cake Garnish is a good accompaniment to a bowl of broth, especially when we have cold weather ahead of us.

6-8 SERVINGS

⅓ cup (50 grams) Wondra flour or hard red wheat flour

1½ tablespoons (20 grams) unsalted butter

Pinch of nutmeg, ground

Pinch of Diamond Crystal Kosher salt

4 large eggs

- Preheat oven to 350° F (175° C).
- Separate egg whites from yolks.
- In a mixing bowl beat butter, yolks, and salt on high speed.
- In a separate bowl, whip the egg whites to a peak.
- Set the mixer on low speed and alternate adding flour and whipped egg whites spoon by spoon into the egg yolk mixture.
- Grease a 9-inch baking pan, dust with flour, and pour the egg batter over it about ½ inch high.
- Bake for 15 minutes or until the sponge cake is nice and golden.
- Let cool and cut into diamond shape pieces.

Egg Omelet Noodles

Omeletové nudle

This simple recipe for noodles made out of eggs adds nutritional value to your soup.

4-6 SERVINGS

3 eggs

Pinch of Diamond Crystal Kosher salt

Pinch of dried parsley, cilantro, or tarragon

3½ tablespoons (50 grams) unsalted butter

- Whisk eggs.
- Add salt and herbs.
- In a skillet with butter, make an omelet.
- Roll the omelet and slice into noodles about ¼ inch (0.6 cm) wide.

Liver Dumplings

Játrové Knedlíčky

Liver Dumplings, or in Czech *Játrové Knedličky*, are essential for a delicious beef broth. They will deepen the flavor of your broth and bring the soup to another level.

6-8 SERVINGS

1 pound (450 grams) chicken liver

½ cup (80 grams) onions, diced

1 egg

1 teaspoon (3 grams) Diamond Crystal Kosher salt (if using another brand, start with about half this amount and adjust to taste).

1 teaspoon (2-2.5 grams) black ground pepper

1 tablespoon (9 grams) garlic, minced

2 tablespoons (4 grams) dried marjoram

1¾ cups (200 grams) breadcrumbs

- Rinse and remove large veins from the livers.
- Run the liver and onions together through a meat grinder.
- In the bowl of a stand mixer fitted with a paddle attachment, add ground chicken liver with onions, egg, salt, pepper, garlic, and marjoram, and mix thoroughly on low speed, about 2 minutes.
- Add breadcrumbs. The dough should be a little sticky. If the dough is too wet, add more breadcrumbs.
- Use a small spoon to pick the dough, and with wet hands, form ¾-inch (2-centimeter) dumplings.
- Refrigerate if they are not to be used immediately.
- Cook them in your broth for 3–5 minutes, or until they rise to the surface.

Croutons

Krutony

These are good added to soups or salads.

4-6 SERVINGS

2 slices of bread, cubed

3½ tablespoons (50 grams) unsalted butter

Pinch of garlic salt

- In a skillet, melt butter on medium-high.
- Add cubed bread and season it.
- Croutons are done when they are golden-brown.
- Use them fresh.

5 Dumplings

Knedlíky

Dumplings were almost certainly discovered in medieval times by someone who made a mistake while making ordinary bread. A story says that the first person responsible for cooking a dumpling was a military chef whose oven was destroyed before he had baked his bread dough. He couldn't think of anything better than to cook it in water.

But as to where they originated, it is impossible to say. It is not surprising that there are arguments among Czechs, Austrians, and Germans over the origin of this gastronomic national treasure. Common heritage has no linguistic or territorial differences.

While the Czech Republic makes dumplings in the shape of cylinders, round-shaped dumplings predominate in Austria and Germany. There are lots of dumpling stories and legends. One tells of the German city Deggendorf, whose nickname is the "City of Dumplings."

It was the time of the siege of Deggendorf by the army of the Czech King Přemysl Otakar II, which allegedly took place in 1266. The siege of the city was long and tiring. One of the Czech soldiers climbed the walls to find out what the defenders were doing. An angry woman threw a dumpling at him, and he was knocked off the wall. The woman's desperate throw to make the siege retreat was brave, because this dumpling had been cooked from the last scraps left in the city.

And it worked. The Czechs decided that there must still be large supplies of food in the city since people could be throwing the food, and they withdrew the attack.

While the legend appears to be over seven hundred years old, in fact it originated in the second half of the nineteenth century. It has undergone several changes; one version is attributed to the Hussite troops.

All Czechs know that when you are served dumplings, the question will arise: will you be served four or six? It is normal to serve four dumplings with a dish, but sometimes the person serving you gives you extra dumplings, which means that you look like a six-dumpling man—a person with a big appetite and room for bigger meal!

Just be careful because it is also a derogatory expression when somebody is on the heavy side. People would tease them for being a *Knedlík*.

Small versions of dumplings are known as gnocchi and spätzle.

Czech Bread Dumplings

Kynuté Houskové Knedlíky

Imagine a roast pork served with sauerkraut and pasta. Or Sauerbraten in Creamy Sauce (*Svíčková*) with rice. Lots of Czech meals are served with wonderful sauces and natural juices, and this is where Czech bread dumplings play a big role. Their soft, fluffy texture will absorb all of the juices and together with other parts of meal will create an umami bite.

You will love these dumplings and be proud that YOU made them!

6 LOAVES

7 cups (1,000 grams) Wondra flour or hard red winter wheat flour

2 cups plus 3 tablespoon (538 milliliter) milk, warm

1 tablespoon (12 grams) sugar

3 tablespoons (25 grams) active dry yeast

2 large eggs

2½ tablespoons (25 grams) Diamond Crystal Kosher salt (If using another brand, start with about half this amount and adjust to taste).

½ cup (100) milliliters) vegetable oil

½ loaf of white bread, cubed and dried for 3 days in open air

Spray bottle with oil

FOR COOKING DUMPLINGS, use a steamer basket that is inserted into a pot over boiling water. The water must not touch the bottom of the basket.

- In a bowl, combine warm milk, sugar, and yeast. Stir.
- In the bowl of a standing mixer with the hook attachment, combine flour, salt, eggs, and oil.
- Add milk with risen yeast. Mix on slow speed for 4–5 minutes.
- Preheat the oven to 350° F (175° C).
- Meanwhile, place 3-day-old, cubed bread on a baking sheet. Spray it with oil and place it in the oven. Roast for 4–6 minutes.
- Fold warm roasted croutons into the dough.
- Let the dough rise until it doubles in size.
- Form 6 equal-size balls. Let them rise for about 10 minutes.

(continues)

- Once they rise, roll them into a cylindrical shape to fit the basket, about 7 inches (18 centimeters) long. Let them rise again for 10 minutes.
- When water is boiling and dumplings have risen, place one or two dumplings into the steamer basket lined with a clean kitchen towel and steam them, covered with a lid, for 20 minutes. Halfway through, turn the dumplings over.
- Before you take the dumplings out of the steamer basket, pull one out and check for doneness by cutting it in the middle using a sewing thread. If you see that the dough is still raw on the inside, replace in the basket and cook for an additional 2–4 minutes. Check the time when the dumplings are done, and adjust cooking time accordingly. Thicker dumplings will take longer to cook than thinner ones.
- Once the dumplings are done, pull them out of the steamer basket, and with a fork, poke holes through the top of each dumpling to release steam. Smear with oil to prevent dryness.
- Repeat for the rest of dumplings. Don't forget to refill pot with water and bring to boil.
- When they are cool, store in the refrigerator or in the freezer.

WHEN READY TO SERVE, place sliced dumplings in to a clean wet kitchen towel and heat them in a microwave for 2 minutes.

TIP

- *Let the bread dry in the open air. Toasted bread will break up into breadcrumbs and dust, which won't work in this recipe.*
- *When pulling dumplings out of basket pull them out in the towel, then replace the towel.*
- *Using thread to cut dumplings is a very old technique. Put the thread under the dumpling, cross it at the top and tighten it. This way your dumpling will not get squashed by the pressure of cutting with a knife.*

Speck Dumplings

Tyrolské Slaninové Knedlíky

These round dumplings with sauteed onions and bacon have exceptional flavor. You can eat them without a sauce.

As the story goes, mercenary soldiers once entered an inn and wanted a quick, filling meal. The cook had only bread, eggs, butter, bacon, and milk. He mixed those all together, and the first dumpling was made. The Czechs adopted this recipe as their own, but it is popular in many countries throughout Europe.

6 DUMPLINGS

¾ cup (100 grams) onions, medium diced

4 ounces (115 grams) bacon, diced

2 tablespoons (28 grams) vegetable oil

4 ounces (115 grams) ham, diced

12 ounces (340 grams) white bread, cubed and air dried for 3 days

2 eggs, beaten

1 cup (250 milliliters) cold milk

½ cup (30 grams) parsley, chopped

1 tablespoon (10 grams) Diamond Crystal Kosher salt (If using another brand, start with about half this amount and adjust to taste)

2 teaspoons (4 grams) black ground pepper

½ teaspoon (1.5 grams) ground nutmeg

¾ cup (125 grams) semolina flour

Spray bottle with oil

FOR COOKING DUMPLINGS, use a steamer basket that is inserted into a pot over boiling water. The water must not touch the bottom of the basket.

- In a skillet, sauté onions and bacon in oil on medium heat until bacon is lightly crisp, about 5 minutes. Add ham. Stir. Let it cool.
- Spray the cubed bread with oil and place it in the oven set on 350° F (170° C). Toast for 6–8 minutes. Let it cool.
- In a large bowl, incorporate toasted bread, milk, beaten eggs, sauteed onion-bacon-ham mixture, salt, pepper, parsley, nutmeg, and semolina flour. With your hands work it into a dumpling mixture. Let it rest for 15 minutes.
- With wet hands, form six 5-ounce (142 grams) round dumplings.
- Place three dumplings into the steamer basket lined with a clean kitchen towel and steam them, covered with a lid, for 15–20 minutes.
- Repeat for the rest of dumplings. Don't forget to refill the pot with water and bring to boil.
- When they are cool, store in the refrigerator or in the freezer.

WHEN READY TO SERVE, place sliced dumplings into a clean wet kitchen towel and heat them in a microwave for 2 minutes.

Carlsbad Dumplings

Karlovarské Knedlíky

These dumplings originated in a Czech spa town known as Carlsbad (Karlovy Vary), a city well known for healing spring waters that brought visitors from all over Europe. Drinking healthy mineral water and eating good healthy food was expected. Carlsbad dumplings were created to fit this demand—a healthier side dish without heavy fats like bacon or lard.

The recipe for Carlsbad Dumplings is almost identical to the recipe for Viennese Dumplings (*Vídenské Knedlíky Servítkové*) The only difference is that you add fried onions to the dough. The name *Servítkové* (Serviette) came from an old technique for cooking dumplings. Chefs used a towel (serviette) to wrap the dumplings before steaming them. Today we use plastic wrap.

3 LOAVES

14 ounces (400 grams) white bread, cubed and air dried for 3 days

4 eggs, separated

1 cup (250 milliliters) milk, warm to the touch

⅔ cup (150 grams) unsalted butter, melted

1 tablespoon (10 grams) Diamond Crystal Kosher salt (if using another brand, start with about half this amount and adjust to taste)

½ teaspoon (1.5 grams) nutmeg, ground

2 tablespoons (8 grams) parsley, chopped

1 cup (30 grams) scallions, green part, chopped

¾ cup (125 grams) semolina flour

- In a bowl, combine the cubed bread, salt, milk and butter. Stir. Add egg yolks, chopped parsley, scallions, nutmeg, and semolina flour. Stir.
- Gently fold in the beaten egg whites.
- Let this dough rest in the refrigerator for 30 minutes.
- Divide the dough into three equal parts. Roll each part into a loaf about 8 in. long. Wrap each loaf in plastic wrap.
- Poke a couple holes through the plastic wrap.

FOR COOKING DUMPLINGS, use a steamer basket that is inserted into a pot over boiling water. The water must not touch the bottom of the basket.

- Steam the loaves for 20 minutes in the steamer basket lined with a clean kitchen towel and covered with a lid.
- Turn them over when halfway done.
- To check if the dumplings are done, remove one dumpling, remove plastic wrap, and gently cut through the middle of the dumpling. If the dough is still raw inside, replace in the steamer and continue cooking. Check the time when dumplings are done and adjust cooking time accordingly. Thicker dumplings will take more time to cook than thinner ones.
- Once the dumplings are done, pull them out of the steamer, and with a fork, poke holes through the top of each dumpling to release steam.
- When cool, store in the refrigerator or freezer. You can leave plastic wrap on for storage.

WHEN READY TO SERVE, place sliced dumplings in to a clean wet kitchen towel and heat them in a microwave for 2 minutes.

Potato Dumplings

Bramborové Knedlíky

Potato dumplings are the perfect side dish and pair best with any kind of roasted meat like duck, goose, or pork.

There are a hundred variants that can turn a dumpling into a mess. Using my recipe, your potato dumplings will always be perfect.

3 LOAVES

5 cups (1,000 grams) Yukon golden potatoes, measured after boiling with their skin on and then peeled (see instructions below)

¾ cup plus 2 tablespoons (150 grams) semolina flour

2 cups plus (250 grams) Wondra flour or hard red wheat flour

2 eggs

1 tablespoon (10 grams) Diamond Crystal Kosher salt (If using another brand, start with about half this amount and adjust to taste)

- Place washed raw potatoes in the pot and cover them with cold water. Cook them until they are al dente, still a little firm, for about 30–35 minutes.
- Let potatoes cool.
- Peel cooked potatoes and grate them on a fine grater into a mixing bowl.
- Add Wondra and semolina flour, egg, and salt. Knead with your hands into a smooth dough.
- Divide the dough into three equal parts, about 17 ounces (500 grams) each. Roll each part into a loaf about 8 in. long. Wrap each loaf in plastic wrap.
- Poke a couple holes through the plastic wrap.

FOR COOKING DUMPLINGS, use a steamer basket that is inserted into a pot over boiling water. The water must not touch the bottom of the basket.

- Steam for 20 minutes in the steamer basket lined with a clean kitchen towel and covered with a lid.
- When halfway done, turn them over.
- To check if the dumplings are done, remove one dumpling, remove the plastic wrap, and gently cut through the middle.

TIP *The same dough can be used for preparing stuffed dumplings with smoked meat or cracklings. Thicker dumplings will cook more slowly than thinner ones.*

History of Potato Dumplings

As the story goes, Franz Trawniček, an army chef of Czech-Austrian origin, is considered to be the father of potato dumplings. His task was to feed the Czech-Austrian troops of Marshal Joseph Radetzky, who was fighting Napoleon at that time. Supplies, especially flour, were very short, and the chef could not bake Bavarian donuts or dumplings. Soldiers were hungry. Chef Trawniček became inspired by the food that the peasants prepared for pigs. It was a mashed potato mixed with bran and water. The chef brought as many potatoes as possible, added little bit of flour and eggs, and threw the mass into boiling water. In a few minutes, the first potato dumpling floated out, and rest is a history of success.

Hairy Dumplings

Chlupaté Knedlíky

These dumplings are made out of raw potato, shredded on the coarse side of the grater and then cooked. Long shavings of potato sticking out of the dumplings gave them their name. This is a classic Czech side dish that could be described as a cross between potato dumplings and Slovak potato spätzle called *halušky*.

4-6 SERVINGS

2½ cups (400 grams) Yukon golden potatoes, total measure after boiled with the skin on and then peeled (see instructions below)

3½ cups (500 grams) Yukon golden raw potatoes

2 cups (250 grams) Wondra flour or hard red wheat flour

3 eggs

1 tablespoon (10 grams) Diamond Crystal Kosher salt for boiling water (If using another brand, start with about half this amount and adjust to taste)

Chives for garnish

- Place washed potatoes in the pot and cover them with cold water. Cook them until they are al dente, still a little firm, for about 30–35 minutes. Let potatoes cool.
- Peel cooked potatoes and grate them on a fine grater into a mixing bowl.
- Peel raw potatoes and grate them on a coarse grater. Squeeze all the liquid and discard the liquid.
- Combine grated raw potatoes and cooked potatoes together.
- Add salt, eggs and flour. Stir.
- Bring the water in the pot to a boil, add salt.
- With a spoon, form dumplings and place them into the boiling water. Stir so that the dumplings don't stick to the bottom of the pot.
- Remove the dumplings with a slotted spoon.
- Drizzle bacon fat over them so that they will not stick to each other.

SERVE sprinkled with chives.
Excellent when served with venison recipes.

6
Entrees
Hlavní Jídla

Czech entrees are a harmony of flavors. The sauces are what make the entrees stand out. Traditional sauces are a national treasure in Czech cuisine. They all start with good stock and fresh vegetables. The meat in various dishes may be prepared similarly, but the sauces will vary.

Sauerbraten in Creamy Sauce, *Svíčková*, is the most popular, with its own velvety root vegetable sauce. When you are dipping dumplings into a sauce, scoop a small piece of meat and lemon with Chantilly cream, and voilà, you get the umami completed bite.

Other sauces that are really unique are dill, pickle sauce, horseradish sauce, and the tomato sauce invented by the Czechs.

We will always come back no matter where we are for the taste and aroma of the Czech cuisine.

Sauerbraten in Creamy Sauce

Svíčková na smetaně

The name *Svíčková* comes from the word *Svíčka,* meaning, "candle." Originally sauerbraten was made out of beef tenderloin, whose shape resembles a candle.

Beef tenderloin is the most expensive cut of beef and is not affordable to all. As a result, cooks began using a more economical substitution – beef eye of round roast, known to Czechs as *falešná svíčková* (false tenderloin). This cut visually resembles a cylindrical shape of tenderloin, making it an attractive and practical alternative at lower cost.

8 SERVINGS

3 pounds (1,400 grams) beef eye of round roast, rinsed, pat dry, cleaned of fat

2 ounces (50 grams) English bacon (also called back bacon), cut into strips for larding or bacon strips

3 tablespoons (30 grams) Diamond Crystal Kosher salt (If using another brand, start with about half this amount and adjust to taste.)

1 tablespoon (7 grams) fresh ground pepper

½ cup (100 grams) oil for searing

2½ cups (300 grams) carrots, peeled and diced

1½ cups (150 grams) parsnip, peeled and diced

1 cup (100 grams) celery root, peeled and diced or celery stalk, diced

1½ cups (200 grams) yellow onion, peeled and diced

½ cup (115 grams) unsalted butter

1 teaspoon (3 grams) peppercorns

1 teaspoon (3 grams) whole allspice

3 bay leaves

Pinch of thyme

1½ quarts (1.5 liters) cold water

1 cube of chicken bouillon

1 small lemon zest

1 tablespoon (15 grams) yellow mustard

1 cup (250 milliliters) half-and-half, divided

3 tablespoons (35 grams) sugar, or to taste

½ cup (100 milliliters) fresh squeezed lemon juice, divided

2 tablespoons (30 milliliters) white vinegar

Lemon decoration wheel, sliced

Heavy cream, whipped with sugar

Cranberry sauce

1 stem of parsley

- Rinse the meat, pat dry with a paper towel, and lard it with long strips of bacon.
- Rub with salt and pepper.
- In the sauté pan, sear the meat on all sides. Set aside.
- In 6-quart oven-safe pot with butter, sauté on medium-high carrots, parsnip, and celery root (stalk) until the vegetables soften, 6–8 minutes.
- Add onion, and sauté until they are translucent 4–6 minutes.
- Add sugar and cook until sugar slightly caramelizes.
- Add peppercorns, allspice, bay leaf, thyme, lemon zest, and mustard. Stir.
- Add ½ amount of lemon juice and all vinegar. Stir.
- Place the seared meat on the top of vegetables. Carefully add water with the bouillon cube, pouring gently to avoid washing off the seasoning on the meat. Let It cool, then refrigerate overnight or up to 72 hours.

- Preheat oven to 400° (200° C).
- Braise the meat for 1.5 hours or until the meat is tender.
- Remove meat from the pot and let it rest.
- Remove the spices, especially the bay leaf; some of peppercorns and allspice may remain.
- Transfer the sauce with all vegetables to a blender. Add remaining lemon juice and ½ cup of half-and-half. Then blend until smooth.
- Return the sauce to the pot and place it over medium heat. Add the remaining half-and-half and cook for 5–10 minutes, stirring continuously.
- Season it to your taste and keep warm until time to serve. The sauce should be sweet and sour.

SERVE with Czech Bread Dumplings, lemon wheels topped with Chantilly cream, cranberry sauce, and parsley.

CHANTILLY CREAM:

- Whip heavy cream with powdered sugar until peaks form, and spoon it on top of the lemon wheels.

TIP *Larding means to insert strips of bacon in meat before cooking. Make incisions with a sharp knife, and push strips of bacon inside with your fingers.*

Braised Beef in Dill Sauce

Koprová Omáčka

Probably few foods trigger as much passion in people as dill sauce—a signature dish of Czech grandmothers, loved by every child. Prepare the beef as you would for Sauerbraten in Creamy Sauce (p. 82), and serve with dill sauce.

4 SERVINGS

DILL SAUCE:

¼ cup plus 1 teaspoon (60 grams) unsalted butter

⅔ cup (80 grams) all-purpose flour

3 quarts (3 liters) beef and dill stems stock

1 tablespoon (10 grams) Diamond Crystal Kosher salt (If using another brand, start with about half this amount and adjust to taste.)

½ cup (100 grams) sugar

3 tablespoons (45 grams) vinegar

1 cup (250 milliliters) heavy cream

1.75 ounces (50 grams) fresh dill

- In a pot, simmer beef stock from the meat with the stems of dill for 1 hour. Discard dill stems, keep the broth.
- In a small pot, make a light roux.
- Add dill/beef stock to the roux. Stir.
- Simmer for 8–10 minutes.
- Season with salt, sugar, and vinegar. Stir.
- Add heavy cream. Stir.
- Strain the sauce through a sieve.
- Add fresh chopped dill.

SERVE with Czech Bread Dumplings.

Roast Pork, Kraut, and Dumplings

Vepřo, Knedlo, Zelo

This dish represents the essence of Czech cuisine. It brings together three popular ingredients: pork, dumplings, and sauerkraut, and a fourth might be the beer you wash it all down with.

8-10 SERVINGS

5 pounds (2,300 grams) pork Ribeye roast

2 cups (200 grams) onions, sliced

⅓ cup (60 grams) bacon fat

3 tablespoons (30 grams) garlic, minced

1 tablespoon (7 grams) carraway seeds

2 tablespoons (20 grams) Diamond Crystal Kosher salt (If using another brand, start with about half this amount and adjust to taste.)

2½ cups (600 milliliters) cold water

1 tablespoon (8 grams) arrowroot thickener

- Preheat the oven to 375° F (190° C).
- Rub the pork with salt and garlic. Sprinkle with caraway seeds.
- In a roasting pot, sauté onions in bacon fat until golden brown.
- Place the pork on top of the onions and add water.
- Cover with aluminum foil.
- Roast for 2½–3 hours, or until internal temperature reaches 155–160 F (70° C).
- Remove the pork.
- In a blender, mix the pan drippings with arrowroot.
- Place it back into the pot and cook the sauce for an additional 10 minutes, or until the sauce thickens.

SERVE with Czech bread dumplings and sauerkraut.

TIP *Drinking beer slightly warmer (40-50 F) is better for your health than drinking ice-cold beer. At warmer temperatures, the flavor of beer opens up and it will help you digest your food.*

Bohemian Roasted Duck

Pečená Kachna

An absolutely perfect recipe for a beginner cook. The procedure is easy, the ingredients are simple, the effort is minimal, but the result is a perfectly cooked meat—juicy but crisp on the surface.

In 1940 a new fish buffet in Prague opened on Wenceslas Plaza by restaurateur Jindřich Vanha. His restaurant became the destination of many gourmets. He became a good friend with my mother and shared some of his secrets with her. He always used butter to cook his fish, and he suggested to my mother to add a nugget of butter to the duck before roasting.

She taught me that trick, and I am sharing this story with you.

4 SERVINGS

1 whole duck

Diamond Crystal Kosher salt

Caraway seeds

2 tablespoons plus 1 teaspoon (30 grams) unsalted butter, sliced

2 cups (500 milliliters) cold water

- Preheat oven to 375° F (190° C).
- Rinse the duck under cool water and remove giblets from the cavity.
- Cut off the tail, fatty parts of neck skin, and first joint of the wings, leaving the upper part attached to the breast.
- Place the giblets with wings, tail, and neck into a roasting pot.
- Rub salt all over the duck, including inside the cavity.
- Sprinkle caraway seeds on both sides of duck.
- Place the duck, breast side down, on the top of the giblets and trims. Add water carefully so that you will not wash salt and caraway seeds off. Place butter under the bottom part of the wings.
- Roast uncovered for 2½ hours.
- Half way through roasting, turn the duck breast-side up. It is good to baste the duck every 30 minutes.
- When the duck is done, take it out of oven and portion it.
- Cut through the breast bone and back bone first, and then between the breast and leg.
- Strain the drippings, skimming off the fat with a spoon. Place drippings in a pitcher or gravy boat for use at the table.

SERVE with Czech Bread Dumplings and red cabbage.

TIP *When you have leftover juices, refrigerate them. When they congeal, remove the fat on the top. Use the fat for frying or as a spread on bread with salt and onions.*

Chicken Paprika

Kuře na Paprice

According to this recipe, which is a remnant of Austro-Hungarian cuisine, our grandmothers cooked hens that had stopped laying eggs. Today we usually cook the delicate meat of fresh young chickens in creamy sauce, flavored with sweet Hungarian paprika.

4 SERVINGS

1 whole chicken (4 pounds), cut up

3 tablespoons (40 grams) unsalted butter

1 cup (100 grams) onions, sliced

3 tablespoons (20 grams) Hungarian Paprika

3 cups (750 milliliters) chicken stock or water

1 cube chicken bouillon

Diamond Crystal Kosher salt

⅓ cup (80 grams) sour cream, for garnish

SLURRY

1 cup (250 milliliters) half-and-half

¼ cup (35 grams) all-purpose flour

- Whisk cold half-and-half with flour to combine.

- Remove the back bone from chicken and cut it into four pieces. Add these to the sauce while cooking, then discard.
- In a large pot, sauté the onions in butter over medium-high heat until they are light golden brown.
- Stir in the paprika and salt.
- Slowly add chicken broth to the pot and chicken bouillon. Add rinsed chicken pieces.
- Bring just to a boil over high heat, then immediately reduce the heat to medium. Simmer for 30 minutes.
- Using a slotted spoon, transfer chicken pieces to a cutting board and set aside.
- Add mixture of half-and-half with flour (slurry) to the sauce. Blend slurry and sauce with an immersion blender.
- Cook for additional 8–10 minutes until thickened.
- Adjust the seasoning with salt if needed.
- Return chicken to the sauce. Keep warm.

SERVE with dumplings, spätzle, or rice. Add a dollop of sour cream on the top.

Beef Goulash

Hovězí Gulaš

Czech Beef Goulash is a thick stew made with beef, onions, and spices. Goulash is popular throughout Europe, but this version is traditionally Czech. The key for the best-tasting goulash is the ratio of onions to meat—use equal amounts of onions and meat.

4-6 SERVINGS

3 pounds (1,400 grams) sirloin, cubed

13 cups (1,300 grams) onions, sliced

¼ cup (65 grams) bacon fat

2½ tablespoons (25 grams) Hungarian paprika

2 quarts (2 liters) beef stock or water

1 cube chicken bouillon

2 tablespoons (20 grams) Diamond Crystal Kosher salt (If using another brand, start with about half this amount and adjust to taste.)

2 teaspoons (8 grams) black ground pepper

2 tablespoons (18 grams) garlic, minced

3 tablespoons (6 grams) dried marjoram

1 each green, yellow, and red bell peppers, cleaned and cut into squares for garnish

2 tablespoons (20 grams) vegetable oil, for grilling bell pepper garnish

ROUX:

¼ cup (60 grams) unsalted butter

⅔ cup (80 grams) all-purpose flour

- In a large pot, sauté onions in bacon fat on medium-high heat until golden brown. Stir occasionally.
- Add paprika. Stir.
- Add cubed meat. Stir. Coat all meat with paprika mixture.
- Add beef stock or water and chicken bouillon. Stir.
- Simmer on low heat, covered, for one hour, or until the meat is tender.
- Separate meat from sauce and add roux to the sauce to thicken it.
- Add garlic and marjoram, and adjust salt to taste.
- Place the meat back into the sauce.

SERVE with Czech Bread Dumplings. Top with grilled bell peppers and a few slices of raw onion.

TIP *Use a pressure cooker and cook the meat for about 5–10 minutes, starting the time right after you hear the first whistle from the pressure cooker. The flavor in the sauce from the meat will be stronger.*

Sausage Goulash

Buřt Gulaš

With the potatoes, this recipe should be actually called potato goulash, and it is definitely worth a try. It will enchant you with its delicate taste.

4-6 SERVINGS

2½ cups (500 grams) Idaho potatoes, peeled, then rinsed and cubed

2 quarts (2 liters) beef stock

1 cube chicken bouillon

¼ cup (50 grams) bacon fat

5 pieces (3 ounces, 85 grams, each) Kielbasa sausage, cut into 1-inch cubes

1¼ cups (200 grams) onions, sliced

2 tablespoons (14 grams) caraway seeds

1½ tablespoons (15 grams) Hungarian paprika

2½ tablespoons (25 grams) garlic, minced

1 tablespoon (10 grams) Diamond Crystal Kosher salt (If using another brand, start with about half this amount and adjust to taste.)

½ teaspoon (1.5 grams) black ground pepper

1½ tablespoons (2 grams) dried marjoram

ROUX:

¼ cup (60 grams) unsalted butter

⅔ cup (80 grams) all-purpose flour

- In a soup pot, sauté onions and kielbasa in bacon fat on medium-high heat until onions are translucent, 8–10 minutes.
- Sprinkle with caraway seeds. Stir.
- Add paprika. Stir.
- Add beef stock, chicken bouillon, and potatoes. Bring to a boil, immediately reduce the heat to low, and simmer until potatoes are tender, about 20 minutes.
- Add salt and pepper.
- Add roux made from butter and flour.
- Add garlic.

SERVE in a soup bowl with bread.

TIP *After you have peeled and cut the potatoes, cover them with cool water so that they will not turn black while you proceed with the rest of the recipe.*

Potato Dumplings with a Smoked Meat Filling

Knedlíky Plněné Uzeným Masem

Round potato dumplings filled with smoked meat, served on a bed of sauerkraut, and topped with roasted onions are a Czech classic.

8 SERVINGS

2 pounds (900 grams) smoked ham hock or neck

6 quarts (6 liters) cold water

3 bay leaves

Pinch of thyme

6 whole allspice

1 cup (100 grams) onions, roughly chopped

5 cups (1,000 grams) Yukon golden potatoes, total measure after boiled with their skin on and then peeled (see instructions below)

¾ cup plus 2 tablespoons (150 grams) semolina flour

2 cups (250 grams) Wondra flour or hard red wheat flour

2 eggs

1½ tablespoons (15 grams) Diamond Crystal Kosher salt (If using another brand, start with about half this amount and adjust to taste.)

2 tablespoons (16 grams) flour for dusting

⅔ cup (140 grams) bacon fat for caramelizing onions

2 onions, sliced for caramelizing

DIRECTIONS FOR THE HAM HOCK:

- In a stock pot, simmer the first 6 ingredients for 3–4 hours.
- If the broth reduces too low, add more water so that the meat is submerged.
- When the meat is falling off the bones, take it out the broth and let it cool. Don't discard the broth; save it for future dishes.
- Chop the meat into small pieces. Make sure that all the bones and cartilages are removed.
- Sauté onions on medium-high heat until translucent, incorporate the meat, and allow to cool.

DIRECTIONS FOR DUMPLINGS:

- Place washed potatoes in the pot and cover them with cold water. Cook them 30–35 minutes, or until they are al dente, still a little firm. Let the potatoes cool.
- Preheat the double boiler.
- Peel the boiled potatoes and grate them on fine grater into a wide bowl.
- Add semolina and Wondra flour, eggs, and salt. With your hands, work into a dough.
- Transfer the dough onto a floured surface and knead it by hand into a smooth dough.
- Divide the dough into 8 pieces, about 5 ounces (140 grams) each, and press each of them out into 6-inch circles.
- Add the smoked meat to the middle of circle and pull the edges up to create a dumpling.
- Place 4 dumplings in the steamer basket lined with a clean kitchen towel and steam, covered with a lid, for 20 minutes.
- The steamer basket should be inserted into a pot over boiling water. The water must not touch the bottom of the basket.
- To check if the dumplings are done, remove one dumpling and carefully cut through the middle to see if it is cooked through. If not, cook for a couple more minutes.
- When dumplings are cooked, poke holes through the top of each dumpling with a fork to release steam.
- In a sauté pan, caramelize onions in bacon fat. Place them on a paper towel to drain excess fat.

SERVE on the top of a bed of sauerkraut, topped with fried onions.

TIP *There is nothing complicated about them, you just have to be careful about the timing. As the potato dough thins quickly, you must always bring the water to a boil before placing the dumplings in the steamer.*

Where did Schnitzel come from?

Surprisingly, Schnitzel did not originate in Germany nor in Austria, as the name might suggest. It came from Milan, Italy, in the Venetian Hotel Danieli. Marshal Joseph Vaclav Radetzky, one of the most famous Czech military leaders who took part in the defeat of Napoleonic France, tasted the local Lombard specialty—Costoletto alla Milanese—(veal wrapped in a mixture of breadcrumbs and Parmesan).

He liked the dish very much, and wished that he could eat it in Vienna and that the Emperor Francis Josef I himself could taste it as well.

However, the chefs in the imperial kitchen in Vienna did not have any Parmesan cheese, so they decided to secretly wrap the veal steak in flour, eggs, and breadcrumbs, without the Parmesan. The emperor enjoyed it, and the Schnitzel has been prepared for ceremonial buffets ever since.

Georg Decker, *Johann Josef Wenzel Graf Radetzky von Radetz*, ca. 1880. Oil. Heeresgeschichtliches Museum, Vienna, Austria.

Vienna Schnitzel

Videnský Řizek

The simple combination of meat, flour, eggs, and breadcrumbs almost conquered the world. The Vienna Schnitzel has to be made out of veal to be called "Vienna." You can use pork for schnitzel, but then you have to call it "Vienna Style."

4 SERVINGS

4 veal cutlets or pork chops

Kosher salt

⅔ cup plus 2 tablespoons (100 grams) all-purpose flour

3 eggs, beaten with a fork

2 cups (216 grams) breadcrumbs

Clarified butter for frying

- Pound the meat on both sides; season with salt.
- Dip each chop or cutlet into flour, beaten eggs, and then breadcrumbs.
- Fry the schnitzels in clarified butter until golden brown on both sides, about 4–6 minutes.

SERVE with Czech potato salad or mashed potatoes and lemon.

TIP

- *It is best to fry the in clarified butter; lard is also permissible, but in either case, use a pan and never a deep fryer.*
- *The schnitzel should have characteristic ripples. It should not be flat as a pancake.*
- *Several factors contribute to the formation of bubbles. Beaten eggs can have a little bit of egg whites not emulsified. The juiciness of the meat will release steam that will lift up the breadcrumbs.*
- *The most important step is frying; the butter must foam, and the schnitzel needs to have room to move around in the pan.*

Szegedin Goulash

Segedinský Gulaš

The authentic Szegedin Goulash is made with pork, sauerkraut, caraway seed, and Hungarian paprika, from which it gets its name. Szeged, Hungary, because of its geographical location, the long-established agricultural method of harvesting, and the way the paprika is milled and ground, has the greatest paprika. Paprika came to Europe from the East in the seventeenth century. This mysterious vegetable was first used only for decoration. It took 200 years for paprika to become a popular spice. Szegedin Goulash is definitely one of my favorite dishes. Full of flavors and easy to make . . . and kids love it!

6-8 SERVINGS

4 pounds (1,800 grams) pork shoulder, cut into 2-inch cubes and seasoned with salt

1½ tablespoons (15 grams) Diamond Crystal Kosher salt (If using another brand, start with about half this amount and adjust to taste.)

1 cup (150 grams) onions, diced

4 tablespoons (40 grams) pork fat or oil

3 tablespoons (30 grams) Hungarian paprika

2 tablespoons (14 grams) caraway seeds

1½ quarts (1.5 liter) beef or chicken stock

2 pounds (900 grams) sauerkraut, lightly rinsed

1 cup (250 milliliters) half-and-half

2 tablespoons (15 grams) all-purpose flour

- In a pot, sauté onions with caraway seeds in the fat or oil until onions are transparent, 4–6 minutes.
- Stir in paprika.
- Add cubed pork. Stir.
- When the meat is coated by paprika, add a little bit of stock. Stir, then add the rest of the stock.
- Cover the pot with a lid and cook for 30 minutes.
- Add sauerkraut and slurry, and cook UNCOVERED for an additional 10 minutes. Stir occasionally.
- Re-season to taste with salt.

SERVE with Czech Bread Dumplings.

Spanish Birds

Španělské Ptáčky

This recipe goes all the way back to the sixteenth century, when Empress Maria of Spain and her husband Maximillian II, the Holy Roman Emperor and King of Bohemia, lived in Prague. Maria was known for her high expectations when it came to food. Wherever she traveled, she would bring her own cooks from Spain.

One of her culinary specialties was a veal steak probably rolled and stuffed with sardines, egg, onion, and butter, and seasoned with coarsely ground pepper. Little picks, which held the roll together, resembled a little bird leg, and that is how its name, Spanish Birds, was born.

One of Empress's sons, Rudolf II, who also became Holy Roman Emperor, particularly loved this dish, and Spanish Birds became a national dish.

Today Spanish people flock to Prague to get this meal in restaurants.

6 SERVINGS

2 pounds (900 grams) eye of round, sliced into 12 pieces about ¼ inch (6 millimeters) thick

Diamond Crystal Kosher salt

Pepper

¼ cup (60 grams) yellow mustard

3 kielbasa sausages, quartered

3 slices (80 grams) grilled bacon, cut in half

3 large whole dill pickles, quartered

1 red bell pepper, sliced

3 eggs, hard boiled

1 cup (100 grams) onions, sliced for stuffing

1¼ cups (200 grams) chopped onions, for sauce

3 tablespoons (40 grams) oil

1½ cups (300 milliliters) cold water

1 cup (250 grams) pickle juice

Twine

- Preheat oven to 375° F (175° C).
- In a deep roasting pan, sauté onions until golden brown. Set aside.
- Pound the sliced meat to stretch it as much as you can without tearing it. Season the meat with salt and pepper on both sides.
- Spread mustard on one side and in the middle place a sausage, bacon, pickle, red bell pepper slice, ¼ of a hardboiled egg, and slices of onion.
- Roll the meat tightly around the stuffing and secure all the sides with cooking twine so that the bird is nicely compact.
- Add the rolled meat to the pan with the onions.
- Add water and juice from pickles. Cook uncovered in the oven for 2½ hours.
- After the birds are cooked, carefully take them out of the pan and cut off the twine.
- Place all the juices into the blender and blend. Adjust the seasoning with salt and pickle juice to taste.

SERVE with rice. Ladle sauce onto the plate and place the bird cut in two on top.

Braised Peppered Rabbit in Red Wine Sauce

Pepřený Králík na Červeném Víně

Hearty and at the same time easily digestible, rabbit meat delights in a roasting pan full of vegetables. It is fragrant with freshly crushed spices and herbs.

4 SERVINGS

FOR THE STOCK:

4 quarts (4 liters) cold water

1 cube chicken bouillon

The neck bone, the trimmings, the giblets, all remaining pieces from rabbit

2 pounds (900 grams) chicken wings

¾ cup (100 grams) each onion, carrot, parsnip, celery stalk

5 stems parsley

1 bay leaf

8 peppercorns

6 whole allspice

- In a stock pot, combine the rabbit trimmings and chicken wings with onions, carrots, parsnip, celery stalk, bay leaf, allspice, peppercorns, and water.
- Simmer for 2 ½ hours.
- In the last ½ hour, add parsley.
- Strain the stock through a fine mesh sieve. Set aside.

FOR THE RABBIT:

1 rabbit, about 3 pounds (1,400 grams), washed, cut into 4 servings; 2 hinds, 2 front legs, 1 center back cut into 2 pieces

4 ounces (115 grams) bacon, diced

2 tablespoons (28 grams) unsalted butter, for cooking the bacon

Diamond Crystal Kosher salt, ground black pepper

⅓ cup (45 grams) all-purpose flour

½ cup (80 grams) shallots, finely chopped

2 tablespoons (28 grams) unsalted butter

1 teaspoon (3 grams) garlic, minced

2 cups (500 milliliters) red wine (Cabernet)

2 quarts (2 liters) rabbit/chicken stock

¼ cup (60 milliliters) brandy

2 tablespoons (30 grams) currant jelly

1 bay leaf

2 fresh stems of thyme or pinch of dried thyme

1 lemon

- In a skillet, sauté the bacon with butter over medium-high heat, stirring frequently until evenly brown. Remove the bacon, retaining the fat.
- Season rabbit pieces with salt and pepper and dip them in flour. Brown rabbit pieces in the skillet of bacon fat. Remove the rabbit. Drain the fat but save the brown fond on the bottom of skillet.
- In a separate pot, sauté shallots with garlic in new butter until soft and transparent. Stir in brandy, red wine, rabbit stock, and the brown fond from the bottom of the skillet.
- Add bay leaf, rosemary, thyme, lemon peel, and currant jelly. Bring to simmer.
- Return rabbit and bacon pieces to the pot. Cover and place into oven for 1 hour, or until rabbit is tender.
- Remove rabbit and strain the liquid through a fine mesh sieve.
- Stir in lemon juice. Adjust the seasoning with salt and pepper.

SERVE with the sauce, potato cakes, and red cabbage.

(continues)

Beef Stroganoff

Hovězí Stroganoff

The commonly accepted history of Beef Stroganoff is that a French chef who worked for a wealthy family created the dish for a cooking contest in 1891 and named it after his employer, Count Pavel Alexandrovich Stroganov. The thin-sliced pieces of meat, which are characteristic of this dish, were offered to the count because he was old and had bad teeth.

4-6 SERVINGS

2 pounds (900 grams) beef tenderloin, cut into strips

1 cup (30 grams) dry mushrooms

2 cups (500 milliliters) cold water, to soak the mushrooms

2 cups (480 grams) sour cream

2 tablespoons (30 grams) Dijon mustard

1 teaspoon (6 grams) Worcestershire sauce

1 pound (450 grams) fresh mushrooms, sliced

2½ tablespoons (35 grams) unsalted butter, for searing beef strips

1 tablespoon (14 grams) unsalted butter, for making sauce

1 cup (100 grams) onions, sliced

1 tablespoon (4 grams) parsley, chopped

½ cup (125 milliliters) white wine

2 stems of fresh thyme

Diamond Crystal Kosher salt

- Place the dry mushrooms into a container with water for 1½ hours or longer (with enough water to cover the mushrooms).
- In a blender, mix the mushrooms with water into a smooth paste.
- In a bowl, mix sour cream, mustard, Worcestershire sauce, and mushroom paste. Set aside.
- In a sauté pan with butter, sear cut strips of tenderloin with thyme for 4–6 minutes. Sprinkle with salt and pepper.
- Take the meat out of the pan, discard the butter, and set the pan with brown fond aside.
- In this same pan with brown fond, add fresh butter, mushrooms, and onions and cook for 6–8 minutes, or until the onions are translucent. Stir.
- Add white wine to deglaze the roasted fond left at the bottom of the pan. Remove the thyme stems.
- Add the sour cream mixture and warm it up.
- Add seared tenderloin. Stir. Don't cook any more.
- Season it to taste.

SERVE on a bed of spätzle or pasta. Sprinkle with parsley.

Smoked Pork with Horseredish Sauce (Kasseler Rippchen)

Uzená Vepřová Kotleta s Křenovou Omačkou

Horseradish sauce is part of the Czech classic arsenal. Try it; you will love it!

4 SERVINGS

4 smoked pork chops, warmed in boiling water

¼ cup (60 grams) unsalted butter

⅔ cup (80 grams) all-purpose flour

1½ quarts (1.5 liters) of strong stock (Ham Hock Stock)

½ cup (100 grams) sugar

3 tablespoons (45 grams) vinegar

1 cup (250 milliliters) heavy cream

¼ cup (60 grams) fresh grated horseradish

Diamond Crystal Kosher salt

Pinch of white pepper

½ cup (50 grams) sliced almonds, toasted

- In a pot, make light roux using butter and flour.
- Add ham hock stock. Stir.
- Simmer for 10 minutes.
- Strain through a sieve into a new pot.
- Season with salt, sugar, and vinegar. Stir.
- Add horseradish and heavy cream. Stir.
- Cook for an additional 8–10 minutes, until thickened.

SERVE with spätzle and sauerkraut. Drizzle horseradish sauce over the cutlets and sprinkle with roasted almonds.

Braised Rabbit in Cream Sauce

Králík ve Smetanové Omačce

The rabbit in cream sauce the old Czech way will not disappoint you if you are looking for an undemanding recipe for an excellent family lunch.

4 SERVINGS

2 pounds (900 grams) rabbit

7½ tablespoons (100 grams) unsalted butter

1½ cups (200 grams) carrots, peeled, then rinsed and diced

1 cup (150 grams) parsnips, peeled, then rinsed and diced

1 cup (100 grams) celery root, peeled, then rinsed and diced

1¼ cups (200 grams) onions, sliced

2⅓ tablespoons (30 grams) sugar

2 tablespoons (30 grams) vinegar

2 tablespoons (10 grams) Diamond Crystal Kosher salt (If using another brand, start with about half this amount and adjust to taste.)

5 bay leaves

Pinch dried thyme

Peel of ½ of lemon and juice from whole lemon

8 black peppercorns

6 whole allspice

2½ quarts (2.5 liters) cold water

1 cube chicken bouillon

⅓ cup plus 1 tablespoon (50 grams) all-purpose flour for coating the rabbit

¼ cup (60 grams) sour cream

- Rinse the rabbit and rub it with salt. Set aside.
- In a pot with butter, sauté carrots, parsnip, and celery until the vegetables soften, 6–8 minutes.
- Add onions, and cook until they are translucent, 3–5 minutes.
- Add sugar, vinegar, salt, bay leaves, thyme, lemon peel and juice from the lemon, black peppercorns, and whole allspice.
- Coat rabbit in flour and add it to the seasoned vegetable mixture.
- Add water and chicken bouillon. Stir.
- Simmer on the top of the stove for 90 minutes, or until the rabbit is tender. Stir occasionally.
- Remove rabbit and place on serving dish. Discard bay leaves and allspice. Add sour cream to the sauce and, with stick blender, blend everything into a smooth sauce. Pour over the rabbit.

SERVE with Schupfnudeln.

Story of St. Martin of Tours

November 11 is the day of celebrating St. Martin of Tours. He was the son of a Roman soldier and was supposed to continue the heritage of his father as a soldier. But he was a kind man who wanted to live a quiet and simple life. He became a monk, hiding from the world so that the soldiers would not find him. The important legend of his life is that while riding his white horse, he cut his cloak in half to share with a beggar who had almost died from the cold. Stories about his kind gesture spread around. Unfortunately, when soldiers heard the story, they began searching for him. He hid in a stable filled with geese. The noise made by the geese betrayed his location, and he was captured.

Josef Lada (1887—1957), *St. Martin*, 1939.
Reprinted by permission from the Lada family.

St. Martin Goose

Martinská Husa

In the Czech Republic and in Germany, people start the celebration of St. Martin on the eleventh month, eleventh day, eleventh hour, and eleventh minute.

It is customary to cook and eat a St. Martin Goose from this day until Christmas. Most of the time, the goose is offered in Czech restaurants every weekend. In Germany, Martin's Goose is eaten on Christmas Eve. It is traditionally served with red cabbage and dumplings.

4-6 PORTIONS

1 goose

Diamond Crystal Kosher salt

2 tablespoons (14 grams) caraway seeds

2 quarts (2 liters) cold water

- Set oven to 375° F (190° C).
- Rinse the goose under cool water and remove giblets from the cavity.
- Cut the wings, tail, and neck off.
- Place the giblets with wings, tail, and neck into a roasting pot.
- Rub the goose, including the cavity, with salt.
- Sprinkle caraway seeds on both sides of the goose.
- Place the goose breast down on the top of the giblets and trims. Add water carefully so that you do not wash the salt and caraway seeds off the bird.
- Cover with aluminum foil and roast for 3½ hours.
- Halfway through roasting, turn the goose so that the breast is up. It is good to baste the goose every 30 minutes.
- When the goose is done, remove from the oven and portion it.
- Cut through the breast bone and back bone first and then between the breast and leg.
- Strain the juices, skimming off fat with a spoon, and pour into a gravy boat or pitcher.

SERVE with Czech Bread Dumplings and red cabbage. Use the juices as a sauce.

TIP *When you have leftover juices, refrigerate them, and when they congeal remove the fat on the top. Use the fat for frying or as a spread on bread with salt and onions.*

Pork Shank (Schweinshaxe)

Vepřové Koleno

The shank is always served whole, and it is usually accompanied by sauerkraut, braised red cabbage, roasted potatoes, or potato dumplings. It is similar to roast pork in taste, but infused with extra flavor and tenderness from still being on the bone.

4 SERVINGS

4 pieces pork shank

1 quart (1 liter) water, cold

1½ cups (200 grams) carrots, peeled, then rinsed and diced

1½ cups (200 grams) parsnip, peeled, then rinsed and diced

⅔ cup (100 grams) celery root, peeled, then rinsed and diced

1¼ cups (200 grams) onions, diced

7½ tablespoons (100 grams) unsalted butter

5 bay leaves

6 whole allspice

8 peppercorns

2 stems thyme

3 tablespoons (27 grams) garlic, minced

Lemon rind from one lemon, plus juice

2½ tablespoons (25 grams) Diamond Crystal Kosher salt (If using another brand, start with about half this amount and adjust to taste.)

- Preheat oven to 375° F (190° C).
- In a roasting pan, sauté carrots, parsnip, and celery root in butter over medium heat for 6–8 minutes.
- Add onions, bay leaves, thyme, lemon peel, allspice, and peppercorns, and sauté until onions are translucent, 3–5 minutes.
- Rub pork shank with salt, garlic, and pepper.
- Place the pork shank in the pot with roasted vegetables and add water.
- Squeeze lemon over the meat and add the rind to the sauce.
- Cover the pot and cook in the oven for 3½ hours.
- Remove the pork shank and set aside.
- Strain the sauce. Remove allspice and bay leaves from strained vegetables.
- Reserve half of vegetables for serving and puree the other half in a blender into a smooth sauce.

SERVE with mashed potatoes. Prop the pork shank up and drizzle the sauce around it. Place the whole vegetables on the top of the sauce.

Christmas Fried Walleye

Vanoční Smažený Kapr

Can you believe that there are 21,000 lakes in the Czech Republic? Yes, this a tiny country with everything big! Carp in the Czech Republic is a symbol of wealth. My mother used to put scales into her wallet for good luck. She would buy carp the day before Christmas Eve and keep the fish in our tub!

The Czech carp is not available in the United States, but walleye is a cousin of carp, and that is why we use walleye for this recipe.

4 SERVINGS

2 pounds (900 grams) walleye

Flour

5 beaten eggs

Bread crumbs

Diamond Crystal Kosher salt

Oil for frying

- Rinse the fish, remove the skin, and portion it.
- Season each filet with salt on both sides.
- Dip into flour, then beaten egg, then breadcrumbs.
- Fry the pieces of fish in oil on medium-high heat until golden brown on both sides, 4–6 minutes.

SERVE with lemon, Czech potato salad, or mashed potatoes.

Beef and Lamb Meatloaf

Sekaná z Hovězího a Skopového Masa

This recipe is my own spin on meatloaf. The mix of beef and lamb is a succulent combination. Adding vegetables adds a perfect balance and makes for juicy meat. Slices of leftover cold meatloaf make good sandwiches for travel. Spread homemade bread with mustard and add the meatloaf slices, pickles, and onions, and your vacation can start.

8-10 SERVINGS

¾ cup (100 grams) onions, sliced

1 green, yellow, or red bell pepper, seeded

6 slices (100 grams) white bread, cubed

1 cup (215 milliliters) beef stock for soaking the bread

2 eggs

2½ pounds (1,150 grams) ground beef

2½ pounds (1,150 grams) ground lamb

1½ tablespoons (15 grams) Diamond Crystal Kosher salt (If using another brand, start with about half this amount and adjust to taste.)

1 teaspoon (2-2.5 grams) ground black pepper

1 tablespoon (9 grams) garlic, minced

8 ounces (225 grams) bacon strips

- Preheat oven to 375° F (190° C).
- In a pan, sauté onions with bell peppers on medium heat until they are tender, 10–15 minutes. Cool.
- Dip the bread in beef stock and squeeze out the liquid. Add the eggs to the bread and blend all together with a stick blender.
- In a large bowl, with your hands, work together the beef and lamb meat, salt, pepper, garlic, egg-bread blend, and bell pepper–onion mixture.
- Form two loaves.
- Place each on a sheet of parchment paper lined with strips of bacon.
- Roll up each loaf with parchment paper in aluminum foil, and fold over the ends of the foil three or four times to seal.
- Bake for 45 minutes, then rotate the pan 180 degrees, and cook for an additional 45 minutes.

SERVE with mashed potatoes and sauerkraut.

Cabbage Rolls

Zelné Závitky

Meat rolled in cabbage leaves is a well-loved dish not to be forgotten.

4-6 SERVINGS

4 quarts (4 liters) cold water for cooking cabbage

1 head white cabbage, cored

2 pounds (900 grams) ground pork

½ pound (250 grams) ground beef

2 tablespoons (30 grams) vegetable oil

¾ cup (100 grams) onions, diced for meat mixture

1 tablespoon (7 grams) Hungarian paprika

3 tablespoons (27 grams) garlic, minced

2 teaspoons (6 grams) Diamond Crystal Kosher salt (If using another brand, start with about half this amount and adjust to taste.)

1 teaspoon (2-2.5 grams) ground black pepper

1 tablespoon (7 grams) caraway seeds, ground

½ cup cooked rice (100 grams)

1 quart (1 liter) cabbage broth, reserved from cooked cabbage

3 tablespoons (45 grams) vinegar

2 tablespoons (25 grams) sugar

1 tablespoon (8 grams) all-purpose flour

- Preheat the oven to 400° F (200° C).
- Bring water with salt to a boil and add the whole cored cabbage head. Cook 3–4 minutes. Pull the cabbage out of the water, reserving the cabbage stock. The outer leaves of the cabbage are now soft and manageable.
- Sauté the onions in oil over medium heat until they are translucent, 6–8 minutes. Stir in Hungarian paprika and allow to cool.
- In a large bowl, combine ground pork and beef, garlic, salt, pepper, caraway, rice, and cool onion-Hungarian paprika mixture.
- Carefully remove outer leaves of cabbage and flatten them on a cutting board or clean work surface.
- Form 3-ounce rolls (85 grams) and place on flattened cabbage leaves.
- Roll each cabbage leaf tightly, tucking in the ends to secure the meat.
- Chop the leftover cabbage and place it on the bottom of a casserole dish. Add salt, pepper and caraway.
- Place cabbage rolls, seam down, on top of the cabbage and add 1 quart (1 liter) of cabbage broth.
- Cover pan with aluminum foil and cook for 45 minutes.
- Remove cabbage rolls and set aside.
- Add vinegar and sugar to the remaining cabbage mixture, cover and cook on medium heat for an additional 10 minutes.
- Place one half of the mixture into a blender, add flour, and purée.
- Add to the remaining half of the cabbage and cook, covered, for an additional 10 minutes.

SERVE cabbage rolls with the remaining cabbage and boiled potatoes.

Stuffed Green Bell Peppers

Plněné Papriky

Stuffed bell peppers are a dish that is popular in the Czech cuisine but are found in kitchens around the world. Bell peppers originated in the Americas and came to the Iberian Peninsula with Columbus's voyages. During the first voyage of Columbus, the person in the crow's nest who yelled "Land, land, land" was someone named Rodrigo de Triana, an ancestor of my husband Jimmy.

6 SERVINGS

6 green bell peppers, seeded

1 cup (50 grams) white bread, cubed

1 cup (250 milliliters) chicken stock, for soaking the bread

3 eggs

2 pounds pork (900 grams), ground

3 tablespoons (27 grams) garlic, minced

½ cup (50 grams) onions, finely diced

2 teaspoons (6 grams) Diamond Crystal Kosher salt (If using another brand, start with about half this and adjust to taste.)

½ teaspoon (1.5 grams) ground black pepper

JASMINE RICE:

1 cup (200 grams) jasmine rice

3 tablespoons (40 grams) vegetable oil

3 cups (715 milliliters) chicken stock, warm

½ cup (50 grams) carrots, peeled, then rinsed and small diced

6 stems fresh cilantro

2 teaspoons (6 grams) Diamond Crystal Kosher salt (If using another brand, start with about half this amount and adjust to taste.)

- In a wide pot, warm up the rice in the oil.
- Add 2 cups stock, diced carrots, cilantro, and salt.
- Cover the pot and cook for 8 minutes on medium-high heat.
- After 8 minutes, stir the rice and add one more cup of warm stock.
- Cook covered for an additional 4 minutes, or until the rice is tender.

BELL PEPPERS:

- Dip the bread in stock and squeeze out the liquid. Add the eggs to the bread and blend all together with a stick blender.
- In a large bowl, with your hands, work together the meat, garlic, onions, half of the amount of rice, salt, pepper, and bread mixture.
- Fill the bell peppers with this mixture.

SAUCE:

1¼ cups (200 grams) onions, sliced

3 tablespoons (40 grams) unsalted butter

5 bay leaves

2 stems fresh thyme or ½ teaspoon dried thyme

6 whole allspice

8 peppercorns

7 cloves

1 teaspoon (2.5 grams) ground cinnamon

1 tablespoon (10 grams) Diamond Crystal Kosher salt (If using another brand, start with about half this amount and adjust to taste.)

⅓ cup (40 grams) sugar

1 lemon peel, cut into strips

⅓ cup (40 grams) all-purpose flour

1 28-ounce can (794 grams) peeled tomatoes, pureed

3 quarts (3 liters) stock or water

¾ cup (170 grams) tomato paste

(continues)

- Set the oven to 350° F.
- In a large roasting pan, sauté onions in butter until translucent, 6–8 minutes.
- Stir in bay leaves, thyme, allspice, peppercorns, cloves, cinnamon, salt, sugar, and lemon peel.
- Stir in all-purpose flour.
- Stir in pureed tomatoes and tomato paste.
- Place filled bell peppers on top of this foundation.
- Add beef stock, cover the pan with aluminum foil, and bake for 1½ hours.
- Carefully take the bell peppers out and remove the bay leaves, peppercorns and allspice from the remaining sauce.
- Puree the sauce in a blender until smooth.
- Return the sauce to the roasting pan and simmer for an additional 10 minutes, then pour into a pitcher or gravy boat.

SERVE with sauce and remaining jasmine rice.

Venison Schnitzel Burger

Jelení Hamburgrový Řizek

I have never shot a hog or deer, but I can butcher a whole animal in no time. So when you have your animal ready for portioning, think of this recipe I created for hunters in Texas. Antelope would be a good for substitution for venison.

10 SERVINGS

5 pounds (2,270 grams) venison shoulder, ground

5 ounces (150 grams) slices of bread

1 cup (250 milliliters) seasoned stock (stock seasoned with salt)

2 eggs

1½ tablespoons (15 grams) Diamond Crystal Kosher salt (If using another brand, start with about half this amount and adjust to taste.)

1 tablespoon (7 grams) ground black pepper

1 tablespoon (9 grams) garlic, minced

⅔ cup (100 grams) all-purpose flour, for breading

3 eggs, beaten with fork, for breading

2 cups (216 grams) breadcrumbs, for breading

- Soak the bread in seasoned stock and squeeze the liquid out.
- Add the eggs to the bread and blend all together with a stick blender.
- Add this mixture to the meat.
- Add salt, pepper, and garlic and mix all together by hand.
- Form 8-ounce (227 grams) patties.
- Dip each patty in flour, then egg, then breadcrumbs.
- Fry the venison schnitzel in clarified butter 4–6 minutes on each side, or until both sides are golden brown.

Venison Ragout in Plum Sauce

Jelení Ragu v Povidlové Omačce

Venison ragout is even better the next day than it is right after cooking, but the aroma and robust flavor with oriental notes make it almost impossible to wait for the next day. Therefore, I recommend cooking ragout for 6-8 people even though you will need only 4 portions. It is a recipe you will love!

6-8 SERVINGS

3 cups (400 grams) onions, sliced

¼ cup (60 grams) pork fat or butter

5 pounds (2270 grams) venison shoulder, cut into 2-inch cubes

1½ tablespoons (15 grams) Diamond Crystal Kosher salt (If using another brand, start with about half this amount and adjust to taste.)

1 teaspoon (2-2.5 grams) black ground pepper

1 teaspoon (2.5 grams) ground cinnamon

Orange zest from one orange, plus juice

2 quarts (2 liters) beef stock

¾ cup (170 grams) tomato paste

⅓ cup (100 grams) plum jam

- In a large pot, sauté onions in bacon fat or butter on medium-high heat 8–10 minutes or until golden brown, stirring occasionally.
- Add cubed meat, salt, pepper, cinnamon, orange zest, and juice from the orange. Stir.
- Stir in stock and tomato paste.
- Cook, covered, over low heat for 1½ hours, stirring occasionally.
- Add plum jam. Stir and cook for an additional 10 minutes. If the sauce gets too thick, add some stock or water and adjust seasoning to taste.

SERVE with Croquettes.

Wild Boar in Rose Hip Sauce

Divočák v Šípkové Omáčce

When my Czech chefs come to visit me, all the guests in my restaurant know that wild game will be served. After we pick up a whole animal from my favorite local supplier, the Broken Arrow Ranch, it is time to prepare all the different cuts for different dishes.

6-8 SERVINGS

5 pounds (2,270 grams) boned leg of wild boar

8 strips (100 grams) bacon, for larding

Diamond Crystal Kosher salt

fresh ground pepper

1½ cups (200 grams) carrots, peeled, then rinsed and sliced

¾ cup (100 grams) parsnips, peeled, then rinsed and sliced

½ cup (60 grams) celery root, peeled, then rinsed and sliced

1 cup (150 grams) yellow onions, sliced

⅔ cup (150 grams) unsalted butter

3 tablespoons (39 grams) sugar

3 bay leaves

Pinch of thyme

8 peppercorns

6 whole allspice

4 juniper berries

2 quarts (2 liters) water or stock

2 cups (500 milliliters) red wine

1 cup (250 milliliters) strong rose hip tea extract (2 tea bags)

12 ounces (340 grams) rose hip jam

½ cup (118 milliliters) lemon juice

⅓ cup (60 grams) butter roux

- Preheat oven to 400° F (200° C).
- Rinse the meat and lard it with long strips of bacon.
- Rub with salt and sprinkle with pepper.
- In a sauté pan, sear the meat on all sides. Set aside.
- In a roasting pan with butter, sauté carrots, parsnips, and celery root on medium-high heat until the vegetables soften, 6–8 minutes.
- Add onions and cook until they are translucent, 4–6 minutes.
- Add sugar, bay leaves, thyme, peppercorns, whole allspice, and juniper berries.
- Add seared meat and cover it with roasted vegetables.
- Carefully add red wine, rose hip tea, and water without washing the vegetables off the meat.
- Braise the meat for 3 hours, or until it is tender.
- Remove the meat and let it rest.
- Remove the bay leaves, allspice, and juniper berries from the pan juices.
- Puree the juices with the butter roux in a blender.
- Return the sauce to the pot and stir in rosehip jam and lemon juice.
- Season to your taste. The sauce should be sweet and sour.

SERVE with Potato Dumplings, Schupfnudeln, Croquettes, or any potato side recipe.

7
Side Dishes
Přílohy

Side dishes complement the main entree and should be chosen to balance it, providing more complete nutrition and creating a harmony of flavors. Choose from a very wide range of recipes, and experiment with them if you want to add a little fun. The most common side dishes in Czech cuisine are dumplings and bread, and these recipes can be found in their own chapters. Here you will find recipes for dishes such as spätzle and potato cakes.

Spätzle

Noky (Falešné Halušky)

The name most likely comes from the German word *Spatzen*, which means "little sparrows." I will describe Spätzle as a fresh pasta that contains the same ingredients as pasta—all-purpose flour, semolina flour, eggs, salt, and water, but it is cooked immediately in salted water.

Why the name *Falešné Halušky*, "False Halušky"? Because spätzle look like *halušky*, a Slovak potato spätzle. The difference is that spätzle are made with flour instead of potatoes.

4-6 SERVINGS

6 eggs

1 cup (250 milliliters) cold water

1½ tablespoons (15 grams) Diamond Crystal Kosher salt (If using another brand, start with about half this amount and adjust to taste.)

2½ cups (300 grams) all-purpose flour

1½ cups (225 grams) semolina flour

6 quarts (6 liters) cold water

1 tablespoon (10 grams) Diamond Crystal Kosher salt for boiling water

- In a mixing bowl, stir first 5 ingredients together. Let the dough rest at room temperature for 20 minutes.
- Bring a large pot of water to a boil; add salt.
- Press the dough through the spätzle maker into boiling water and boil for 10 minutes, stirring occasionally.
- While the spätzle cooks, fill a large bowl with water and add enough ice cubes to keep the water ice-cold for at least 15 minutes.
- Lift the spätzle out of the boiling water with a slotted spoon, and immediately plunge them into the ice water. Drain thoroughly.
- Store in the refrigerator.

Now you can be creative!

ADD sauerkraut and cheese, or mix into sautéed vegetables, or serve as is as a side.

Almond Croquettes

Mandlové Krokety

Another classic Czech recipe. Croquettes are a type of dumpling consisting of a thick batter made out of potatoes, eggs, and flour, which is then breaded and fried.

4-6 SERVINGS

2½ cups (300 grams) Wondra flour or hard red wheat flour

1½ cups (300 milliliters) water

⅔ cup (150 grams) unsalted butter

Pinch of Diamond Crystal Kosher salt

3 cups (500 grams) potatoes

4 eggs

1 cup (100 grams) sliced blanched almonds

1¾ cups (250 grams) all-purpose flour

4 eggs for breading

2⅓ cups (250 grams) bread crumbs

Bacon fat or duck fat for frying

- Place washed potatoes (with skin) in a medium-large pot and cover with cold water. Cook 30–35 minutes, or until they are al dente, still a little firm.
- Let the potatoes cool, then peel and grate on a fine grater.
- In a pot, bring water, salt, and butter to a boil, stirring constantly.
- When the water is boiling, add flour and reduce heat to low.
- With a wooden spoon, keep stirring the dough for 3–4 minutes, or until it does not stick to the sides of the pot. The cooked dough will leave a white film behind.
- Let the dough cool. Remove from the pot and place in the bowl of a stand mixer with the paddle attachment.
- Add eggs. Mix.
- Mix in grated potatoes and half the almonds.
- With wet hands, form 2-ounce (57 grams) balls (about 2 heaping tablespoons each).
- Roll the balls in flour to create 4-inch long logs.
- Dip the logs in eggs and then in bread crumbs mixed with the remainder of the almonds.
- Fry the croquettes in the fat until golden brown.
- Drain on paper towels.

SERVE as a side with a variety of meals.

Schupfnudeln

Šulánky

"Finger shaped potato noodles" served in Germany usually fried as a side to accompany the entrée.

The Czechs serve Schupfnudeln fried as well, but sometimes they like to boil *Šulánky* in sweet water and serve them with ground poppy seeds, powdered sugar, and melted butter as a dessert.

2.2 pounds (1000 grams) Yukon golden potatoes

2½ cups (300 grams) all-purpose flour

2 eggs

Diamond Crystal Kosher salt, pepper

Pinch of nutmeg

Clarified butter for frying

- Place washed potatoes (with skin on) in a pot and cover with cold water. Cook 30–35 minutes, or until they are al dente, still little firm.
- Let the potatoes cool, then peel and grate into a mixing bowl.
- Add salt, eggs, flour, pepper, and nutmeg.
- Knead until dough is smooth.
- On a floured work surface, form long rolls. Cut them into 4-inch-long sticks.
- Shape each stick with your floured fingers into a finger noodle.
- Fry in clarified butter until golden brown.

SERVE with any Czech dish as a side instead of dumplings.

USE the same recipe and finish it as a sweet dish, as the headnote explains.

Potato Cakes

Bramborové Placky

Potatoes are one of the basic ingredients of Czech cuisine. They can be used to make all kinds of delicacies, even sweet ones.

This recipe will bring back what our grandmothers knew how to make, but unfortunately many of us have forgotten the dish.

4-6 SERVINGS

18 ounces (500 grams) Yukon golden potatoes

1¼ cups (150 grams) Wondra flour
or hard red wheat flour

1 egg

1 teaspoon (9 grams) garlic salt

1 teaspoon (3 grams) Diamond Crystal Kosher salt (If using another brand, start with about half this amount and adjust to taste.)

1 tablespoon (15 grams) unsalted butter, softened

Duck fat for frying

- Place washed potatoes (with skin on) in a large pot and cover with cold water. Cook for 30–35 minutes, or until they are al dente, still a little firm.
- Drain and allow to cool.
- Peel and grate the potatoes on a fine grater into a mixing bowl.
- Add flour, egg, garlic salt, Kosher salt, and softened butter.
- Form 5-ounce (57 grams) balls (approximately a rounded ⅓ cup each). Flatten with your fingers to create disks.
- Fry in duck fat.

SERVE as a side or as a dessert dish with jam and Chantilly cream.

Warm Spätzle Salad

Teplý Nokový Salát

What side dish will we refresh the menu with today? Any pasta is warmly welcome, so for a change, we will offer the hungry family spätzle mixed with cheese and bacon bits.

4-6 SERVINGS

SPÄTZLE

6 eggs

1 cup (250 ml) water, cold

1½ tablespoons (15 grams) Diamond Crystal Kosher salt (If using another brand, start with about half this amount and adjust to taste.)

2½ cups (300 grams) all-purpose flour

1½ cups (225 grams) semolina flour

6 quarts (6 liters) cold water

1 tablespoon (10 grams) Diamond Crystal Kosher salt for boiling water.

- In the bowl of a stand mixer with a paddle attachment, mix first five ingredients together. Let the dough rest for 20 minutes.
- Bring the 6 quarts of water to a boil in a large pot and add salt.
- Press the batter through the spätzle maker into boiling water and boil for 10 minutes, stirring occasionally.
- Lift the spätzle from the boiling water with a slotte spoon and immediately plunge into ice water. Drain in a sieve or colander.
- Store in the refrigerator.

MORNAY SAUCE

2 tablespoons plus 1 teaspoon (30 grams) unsalted butter

¼ cup (34 grams) all-purpose flour

1½ cups (375 milliliters) milk

1 teaspoon (3 grams) Diamond Crystal Kosher salt (If using a different brand, start with about half this amount and adjust to taste.)

½ teaspoon (2 grams) black ground pepper

Pinch nutmeg

5¾ ounces (60 grams, or approximately ¾ cup less a teaspoonful) Gruyere cheese, grated

(continues)

- In a small pot, melt butter over medium heat.
- Add flour. Whisk.
- When the roux starts to turn pale yellow, add milk. Continue whisking until the mixture thickens and forms bubbles.
- Reduce heat to low and simmer for 3-4 minutes.
- Remove from heat and add salt, pepper, and nutmeg.
- Add grated cheese and stir until the cheese melts into the sauce.
- Remove from heat.

SPÄTZLE SALAD

1 cup (100 grams) onions, sliced

½ cup (60 grams) bacon, cut into about 1-inch pieces

- Sauté onions and bacon until bacon is crispy.
- Pour off excess fat. Add spätzle and warm with the onions and drippings.
- Plate the spätzle with bacon and pour the cheese sauce over it.
- Sprinkle with parsley.

SERVE as a side or as a meal.

Spätzle with Ham and Kraut

Nokový Salát se Šunkou a Zelím

For winter weather, spätzle is absolutely ideal. The combination of sautéed onions and ham will fill the room with the aroma of a homemade meal that will stay in your memory.

1 SERVING

1¼ teaspoons (6 grams) unsalted butter

About ⅓ cup (150 grams) diced ham

½ cup (100 grams) onions, small diced

6 ounces (170 grams) of spätzle

Pinch of Diamond Crystal Kosher salt

Pinch black ground pepper

3 heaping tablespoons (85 grams) sauerkraut, or to taste

- In a pan with butter, sauté onions and ham 6–8 minutes, or until onions are translucent.
- Add spätzle and warm them. Season them with salt and pepper.
- Stir in sauerkraut.
- Sprinkle with parsley.

SERVE as a side or as a meal.

8

Salads

Saláty

Veal Vienna Schnitzel served with Czech potato salad and a side of cucumber salad is one of my favorite memories of a Sunday lunch.

Most of the time, salads and entrees are served at the same time. In these days, salads are sometimes preferred as a light meal in the evening.

There is no rule that salads have to be made out of vegetables and starch. In addition to vegetable salads, this chapter contains recipes for some great salads made out of sausages and other kinds of meat.

Czech Potato Salad

Bramborový Salát

A bowl of chilled potato salad belongs to the Christmas traditions in the Czech Republic. Each family has its own favorite recipe, without which the holidays would not be complete.

I prepare the Czech Potato Salad from 2 pounds (900 grams) of potato just for myself. My daughter loves this salad very much too, so for her and me, I double the amount and call it two servings. Find out if you are like me and my daughter!

4-6 SERVINGS

2 pounds (900 grams) Yukon golden potato, cooked with skin on

1 cup (100 grams) each washed carrots, parsnips, and celery root

½ cup (100 grams) onion, small diced

6 tablespoons (100 grams) pickles, small diced

¾ cup (100 grams) defrosted frozen peas or drained canned peas

6 eggs, hard boiled, small diced

About ⅔ cup (150 grams) mayonnaise

1 teaspoon (5 grams) yellow mustard

2 tablespoons (30 grams) lemon juice, fresh squeezed

3 teaspoons (9 grams) Diamond Crystal Kosher salt (If using another brand, start with about half this amount and adjust to taste.)

1 teaspoon (2-2.5 grams) black ground pepper

- Boil potatoes, carrots, parsnips, and celery root together in the same pot with their skins on until the potatoes are tender, about 35 minutes. Do not overcook!
- Peel and dice all the vegetables when they are cool to the touch.
- In a bowl, fold all the vegetables, pickles, peas, eggs, mayonnaise, mustard, and lemon juice together with a spatula.
- Add salt and pepper to taste.

SERVE as a side dish with all different meats.

TIP *Use a baguette cut into 4 pieces and then cut in half. Spread butter on each piece of bread and top it with the Czech potato salad, a slice of ham rolled into a cone shape, a slice of hard-boiled egg, a slice of dill pickle, and a slice of red bell pepper. Sprinkle with Hungarian paprika and add a fleurette of fresh parsley. This kind of open-face sandwich will make Jan Paukert proud of his invention!*

My mother knew him personally and loved him, and who knows how much?

Cucumber Salad

Okurkový Salát

One Sunday when my mother was roasting a chicken for lunch, she asked me to help her to make a dressing for a lettuce salad she wanted to serve with the chicken. I could not have been more than 8 years old and didn't have any idea how it was made. I asked her, "How do I do it?" She replied, "Put sugar, vinegar, and water together, and make it taste good!" You might say: boring, easy! But, believe it or not there is a difference between mixing water and sugar, then vinegar and mixing sugar and vinegar, then water. There is simply something in the steps of making it. It is the same for this cucumber salad recipe. First, season the cucumber with salt and pepper, then add the dressing.

4 SERVINGS

3 cucumbers, peeled and grated

2 teaspoons (6 grams) Diamond Crystal Kosher salt (If using another brand, start with about half this amount and adjust to taste.)

1 teaspoon (4 grams) black ground pepper

- Peel the cucumbers, rinse them after peeling, and shred or grate coarsely.
- Add salt and pepper. Stir.
- Pour the dressing over the cucumbers and stir.

DRESSING

⅓ cup (65 grams) sugar

2 tablespoons (30 grams) vinegar

2 cups (500 milliliters) cold water

- Mix first two ingredients and then add water.

SERVE as a refreshing dish—especially good with Vienna Schnitzel.

Tomato Salad

Rajčatový Salát

The tomato is a native plant of South America. The seeds were brought to Europe in 1600s and were planted as an ornamental curiosity. It took 300 years to overcome the fear of eating the fruit because it was commonly known that the leaves and stalk of the tomato plant are toxic. Everybody assumed that the fruit was poisonous too, and it was nicknamed "poison apple."

4-6 SERVINGS

3¾ cups (500 grams) tomatoes, washed, medium diced

½ cup (100 grams) onions, small diced

2 teaspoons (6 grams) Diamond Crystal Kosher salt (If using another brand, start with about half this amount and adjust to taste.)

1 teaspoon (2-2.5 grams) ground black pepper

2 tablespoons (8 grams) chopped parsley

- Wash the tomatoes and dice them.
- Add onions, salt and pepper. Stir.
- Add dressing. Stir.
- Add parsley.

DRESSING

⅓ cup (65 grams) sugar

2 tablespoons (30 grams) vinegar

2 cups (500 milliliters) cold water

- Mix together all these ingredients.

SERVE with any dish and especially with Vienna Schnitzel.

Salmon Salad

Lososový Salát

I created this salad recipe about twenty-five years ago for the Friday Night Knitting Club held in my knitting and toy shop Ewe and Eye. On Friday nights we would gather together, sip wine, and eat these crazy things I would come up with. This one was the favorite of them all, and later this recipe ended up on our menu at Little Gretel Restaurant.

4-6 SERVINGS

1 pound (450 grams) fresh salmon

1 tablespoon (9 grams) pressed garlic

1 tablespoon (14 grams) olive oil

1½ cups (150 grams) each shallots and celery stalk

1½ cups (150 grams) carrots, peeled, rinsed, grated, and then chopped

½ cup (125 grams) mayonnaise

1 teaspoon (5 grams) yellow mustard

Freshly squeezed juice of 1 lemon

2½ tablespoons (10 grams) chopped parsley

2½ tablespoons (10 grams) chopped cilantro

1 teaspoon (3 grams) Diamond Crystal Kosher salt (If using another brand, start with about half this amount and adjust to taste.)

Pinch of fresh ground pepper

- Preheat the oven to 350° F (175° C).
- Rinse the salmon and pat dry. Place in a roasting pan and rub garlic on the top. Drizzle olive oil over the top.
- Cover with aluminum foil and bake in the oven for 30 minutes.
- Let cool.
- Mince all the vegetables and mix them together with the next 7 ingredients. Stir in cold, flaked salmon.

SERVE as a side dish or on the top of your favorite salad. My Friday night knitting club enjoyed this recipe on the top of a grilled English muffin.

Lentil Salad

Čočkový Salát

Lentils don't have to be served only on New Year. Lentils are a secret superfood! Besides being eco-friendly (they improve soil fertility), they are also economical and rich in protein and fiber.

4-6 SERVINGS

1 pounds (450 grams) lentils

1½ quarts (1.5 liters) water

½ cup (50 grams) carrots, peeled, rinsed, small diced

½ cup (50 grams) celery stalk, small diced

1 cube chicken bouillon

2 tablespoons (8 grams) cilantro leaves, chopped

1 tomato, small diced

½ cup (118 milliliters) vinaigrette dressing

Diamond Crystal Kosher salt to taste

- Rinse lentils under cold running water.
- In a pot, cover lentils with about 2 inches of water and bring to a boil with salt, carrots, celery stalk, and cube of chicken bouillon. Then immediately reduce the heat to medium and cook an additional 15–20 minutes, or until lentils are tender. Drain and allow to cool.
- Add cilantro, tomatoes, and vinaigrette dressing.

VINAIGRETTE DRESSING

¾ cup (175 milliliters) olive oil, or oil of your choice

¼ cup (60 milliliters) red wine vinegar

½ teaspoon (2 grams) Diamond Crystal Kosher salt (If using another brand, start with about half this amount and adjust to taste.)

¼ teaspoon (1.5 grams) black ground pepper

- Mix all the ingredients together. Keep remaining dressing in the bottle or a closed container in the refrigerator for other use.

SERVE as a side dish or enjoy it as a meal.

Farro Salad

Salát ze Špaldy

Farro is an ancient grain that has been around for thousands of years. It is very healthy and easier to digest than all other grains. I love to eat it for breakfast with a dash of virgin olive oil and egg yolk.

4-6 SERVINGS

1 cup (190 grams) Farro grain

1 quart (1 liter) beef stock, for cooking the grain

1 tablespoon (10 grams) Diamond Crystal Kosher salt (If using another brand, start with about half this amount and adjust to taste.)

Pinch of minced garlic

Pinch of ground black pepper

½ cup (100 grams) red beets

1 cup (20 grams) arugula, chiffonade

¼ cup (30 grams) pecan pieces

¼ cup (60 milliliters) vinaigrette dressing (see recipe on previous page)

½ cup (60 grams) feta cheese, crumbled

- Rinse Farro grain under cold running water.
- In a pot, bring the Farro grain and stock with salt to a boil and then immediately reduce the heat to medium. Cook for an additional 30 minutes, or until the grain is tender.
- Quickly drain, rinse with fresh water, and allow to cool.
- Add garlic, salt, and pepper. Stir.
- Add red beets and arugula.
- Add vinaigrette dressing. Stir.
- Sprinkle with feta cheese and pecans.

Beef Tongue Salad

Salát z Hovězího Jazyka

Who said salad has to be made only out of vegetables?

If you have never tried beef tongue before, be ready for a nice surprise! The rich beefy flavor will not disappoint you, and the tender meat will almost melt in your mouth. This recipe is perfect for those who are looking for something delicate to eat.

6 SERVINGS

TONGUE

4 quarts (4 liters) cold water for brine

¾ cup (105 grams) Diamond Crystal Kosher salt (If using another brand, decrease by about half and adjust to taste.)

½ cup plus 2 tablespoons (125 grams) sugar

3 pounds (1,400 grams) beef tongue

7½ tablespoons (100 grams) unsalted butter

2½ cups (300 grams) carrots, peeled, rinsed, and diced

¾ cup (150 grams) parsnips, peeled, rinsed, and diced

⅔ cup (100 grams) celery root, peeled, rinsed, and diced

1¼ cups (200 grams) yellow onions, sliced

2 bay leaves

Pinch of dried thyme

6 whole allspice

8 peppercorns

3 cloves garlic

1 teaspoon (3 grams) Diamond Crystal Kosher salt, for cooking the tongue (If using another brand, decrease by about half and adjust to taste.)

1½ quarts (1.5 liters) cold water, for cooking the tongue

SALAD

12 ounces (340 grams) marinated pearl onions

1 teaspoon (2 grams) Hungarian paprika

2 teaspoons (10 milliliters) soy sauce

1 tablespoon (15 milliliters) Worcestershire sauce

½ cup (115 grams) ketchup

16 ounces (1 jar, 454 grams) roasted red peppers, sliced

(continues)

2 tablespoons (30 grams) prepared yellow mustard

Pinch of Diamond Crystal Kosher salt

¾ cup (100 grams) Claussen Kosher Dill pickles, minced

Fresh baby greens

- Prepare the brine. In a stock pot, combine water with the sugar and Kosher salt. Simmer and stir until salt and sugar are dissolved. Remove from heat and allow to cool.
- Add the tongue to the brine and refrigerate overnight.

- Preheat the oven to 375° F (190° C).
- Remove tongue from the brine and wash well; discard brine.
- In a roasting pan, combine butter, carrots, parsnips, and celery root and sauté until the vegetables soften, 6–8 minutes.
- Add onions and sauté until they are translucent, about 4 minutes.
- Add bay leaves, thyme, allspice, peppercorns, garlic, and 1 teaspoon Kosher salt. Stir.
- Add washed tongue and cover it with roasted vegetables.
- Add water carefully, without disturbing the vegetables. Cover the roasting pan with aluminum foil and roast for 2 hours, or until tongue is tender. Add more water if needed.
- Remove the tongue and allow to cool.
- When tongue is cool enough to handle, peel off the skin and discard. Slice the tongue into strips.
- To assemble the salad, mix pearl onions, paprika, soy sauce, Worcestershire sauce, ketchup, red peppers, mustard, salt, and minced pickles.
- Fold in the strips of tongue.

SERVE on a bed of fresh baby greens.

Kielbasa Salad

Klobásový Salád

With the unexpected combination of flavors and textures, this summer salad will win everybody's heart.

4-6 SERVINGS

4-5 Kielbasas, sliced, without casing

4.5 ounces (1 jar, 127 grams) marinated sliced mushrooms

½ cup (100 grams) cherry tomatoes, cut in half

⅓ cup (50 grams) onions, thinly sliced

1 teaspoon (3 grams) Diamond Crystal Kosher salt (If using another brand, decrease by about half and adjust to taste.)

¼ teaspoon (1.5 grams) ground black pepper

¼ cup (60 milliliters) vinaigrette dressing (see p. 124)

2 tablespoons (42 grams) sliced fresh jalapenos

- In a sauté pan, lightly warm up Kielbasa slices, saving all the juice.
- In a bowl, toss together Kielbasas with juices and other ingredients.

SERVE at room temperature with homemade rolls or bread.

9
Breads
Pečivo

There is an old Czech proverb saying, "How you deal with bread is how you deal with people." My mother taught me to cut bread toward my heart. "As you cut the bread toward your heart, you trust people and you show them that they are welcome to your home," she said. Cutting bread evenly toward your heart means, "You can cope with people."

Bread was basic to diets from ancient times. Until the time of Charles IV, people ground the grain for bread on their own, but in the fourteenth century, mills began to be built on a large scale, and that triggered a change in people's eating habits. A new law was passed, and people could not eat fresh bread because they ate it too fast and would not have any left for the next day. The law required people to save the bread for the next day. Ecclesiastical regulations and observance of fasting were based not only on religious practice but also on practical need. Common people were forced to eat less and make supplies last for times of scarcity.

When the bread was completely hard and could not be eaten, it was used in the kitchen to thicken other dishes or to make a porridge, for example. That method has survived to this day. To our Czech bread dumplings, we add three-day-old cubed white bread. We still have a tradition of toasting small bread cubes and topping soups with them. Bread has also been used to make certain types of soups. The most popular is *oukrop*, a soup prepared from water, caraway seed, garlic, and bread.

People respected bread. In Slavic countries, guests are welcomed with bread and salt. Bakers were one of the highest officials in the royal court. They kept an eye on how festivities progressed and announced when the party or banquet ended.

Baking good bread is not easy affair, and that is why the counselors used to guard the craft and the bakery very strictly. Each baker had their own symbol engraved in his bread so that everyone knew what bakery the bread was from. This would protect their own bakery from others who would cheat. Those who cheated were caught and placed in a wicker cage above the Moldau River, where onlookers could spit on them and throw rubbish and stones. Sometimes bakers would cut the ropes with knifes so that they could escape the torment, and sometimes they would fall into the water and drown.

Czech Superstar Bread

Domací Chleba

When I first came to United States in 1978, I was introduced to this recipe, and since then I have played with it, adding this here and that there. I perfected the recipe to my own taste with salts and seeds in addition to the original caraway seeds. I normally add a couple of tablespoons of flax seed, chia seed, raw pumpkin seed, hemp seed, and sometimes even pork caviar! Try it, and I think you'll be hooked. Just remember that high-quality flour is the most important component.

2 LOAVES

2½ cups (600 milliliters) warm water

1 teaspoon (4 grams) sugar

4 tablespoons (32 grams) active dry yeast

7 cups (1,000 grams) Wondra flour or hard red wheat flour

2 tablespoons (20 grams) Lawry's garlic salt

1 tablespoon (10 grams) Diamond Crystal Kosher salt (If using another brand, begin by using about half this amount, and adjust to taste.)

2 tablespoons (14 grams) caraway seeds

⅓ cup (70 grams) vegetable oil

3 tablespoons (45 grams) white vinegar

Vegetable oil for hands

- In a measuring cup with warm water, add sugar and yeast. Stir and let the yeast proof until foamy, 3–4 minutes.
- In the bowl of a stand mixer fitted with a dough hook, mix all dry ingredients and then add yeast mixture, oil, and vinegar. On low speed, incorporate into a smooth dough (about 4 minutes). The dough should be elastic and easy to take out of the mixing bowl.
- Oil hands and form dough into a large ball on the table, then return it to the bowl. Cover with plastic wrap and let it rise in warm place for 30 minutes.
- Preheat the oven to 400° F (200° C).
- Once the dough doubles in size, form a couple of loaves.
- Place the loaves on a greased baking sheet sprinkled with flour, and let it rise again for about 10 minutes.
- Brush the loaves with water and place them in the oven.
- Bake for 25–30 minutes, or until they are a nice golden brown.

TIP *The time dough takes to rise depends on the temperature of your kitchen. In warmer kitchens, the dough will rise more quickly than in cooler ones. In commercial kitchens, the perfect room temperature is when the baker starts to sweat! Use proofing baskets, also known as bannetons, for creating different shapes for your bread.*

Marionettes: Saving the Czech Language

The act of building marionettes has long been a form of protest for the Czech people. In the seventeenth century, when the kingdom of Bohemia was under Habsburg rule, the Czech language almost disappeared. People's identity and the Czech language were taken away for almost three hundred years. So why don't Czechs speak German?

Seventeenth-century wood carvers, who were more versed in sculpting Baroque seats for churches than human facsimiles, started making marionettes for the actors of Bohemia soon after Ferdinand II came to power and discouraged the Czech language. While the rest of the country and its people adhered to the newly imposed German language, wandering actors and marionette masters spoke through the marionettes in their native Slavic tongue. The marionettes were the only remaining entities that had the right to speak Czech in public places.

It might seem unlikely that a few hundred marionettes and marionette-masters could safeguard a language, especially through a loophole, but the people's last remaining legacy to their past was tied to the puppet's strings. It's easy to see why these marionettes have found a home in Czech hearts, and why the magic of marionettes continues to permeate the city of Prague.

Kaiser Rolls and Czech Crescents

České Domácí Pečivo

There is nothing better than freshly baked bread. An easy recipe may change your mind about making it, and you will never buy commercially made rolls again!

12 PIECES

3½ cups (500 grams) all-purpose flour

1 teaspoon (4 grams) sugar

5 teaspoons (15 grams) active dry yeast

1½ cups (330 milliliters) warm water, divided into 1 cup (220 ml) and ½ cup (110 ml)

2 teaspoons (6 grams) Diamond Crystal Kosher salt (If using another brand, begin by using about half this amount, and adjust to taste).

¼ cup (65 grams) butter, pork butter, bacon, duck, or even goose fat

DOUGH

- In the bowl of a stand mixer fitted with a dough hook, add flour and make a well in the center. To this well add sugar, yeast, and only 1 cup (220 ml) of warm water. DO NOT STIR.
- Cover and let the yeast proof for 30 minutes.
- Add the rest of the water, warm rendered fat, and salt.
- Knead all ingredients together.
- Cover the dough and let rise until the dough doubles in size.
- Form 12 equal-size balls (2.6 ounces or 73 grams each). Let these rise, covered, for 20 minutes.
- Form into Kaiser Rolls or Crescents.

SHAPING KAISER ROLLS

- Roll out each ball of dough in a flat circle about 6 inches (15 cm) in diameter.
- With your fingers pull 5 points away from the center of flat circle and press them to the table. The points are going to try to shrink back to the original position. Quickly with your fingers pull the points toward the center of the circle one by one and press the tips hard to stick to the center of the circle. Press the last point over the four.
- Another way to shape the Kaiser Rolls is with the tip of a scissors. Cut through the top of the flattened ball.
- Or, center a Kaiser stamp over the flattened ball of dough and press down firmly almost to the bottom, but do not cut all the way through.

SHAPING CRESCENTS

- Using a floured rolling pin, roll each ball into a rough triangle, then stretch three corners until you have a triangle with one short and two equally long sides (i.e. an isosceles triangle).
- Roll up by hand, starting from the short side.
- Turn the ends of roll toward each other to form a crescent.

BAKING

- Cover and let the rolls rise for 30 minutes, or until doubled in size.
- Preheat oven to 450° F (220° C).
- Place Kaiser Rolls or Czech Crescents on a lightly greased baking sheet.
- Coat the rolls with egg white, then sprinkle with salt, caraway seeds, poppy seeds, or any other seeds you like.
- Bake 12–15 minutes.

Sourdough Bread

Chléb Kvasový

If you have never made your own starter, this is your opportunity. This recipe will guide you step by step. It is exciting to watch the process of yeast feasting on sugars. It will take about 8 days to grow your starter to perfection. Leftover starter can be refrigerated and used for the next batch of Sourdough Bread.

1 BOULE

4 cups (500 grams) King Arthur unbleached all-purpose flour

¾ cup (200 grams) starter, at room temperature

1 teaspoon (6 grams) Lawry's garlic salt

1 teaspoon (3 grams) Diamond Crystal Kosher salt (If using another brand, begin with about half this amount and adjust to taste).

2 tablespoons (14 grams) each caraway seeds and flex seed

1 tablespoon (10 grams) pumpkin seeds, chia seeds

1¼ cups (300 milliliters) water at 110° F (43° C)

1 tablespoon (9 grams) active dry yeast

1 teaspoon (4 grams) sugar

STARTER

1½ cups (180 grams) all-purpose flour, divided

½ cup (120 ml) room temperature water, to start with

1 tablespoon (21 grams) honey

1 cup (120 grams) rye flour, divided

- Prepare the starter. In a glass bowl with 1 cup (120 grams) all-purpose flour, add ½ cup (120 ml) water and the honey; stir.
- Cover with plastic wrap. Do not refrigerate.
- 3rd day, add ½ cup (60 grams) rye flour and ¼ cup (60 ml) water; stir.
- 5th day, add ½ cup (60 grams) all-purpose flour and ¼ cup (60 ml) water; stir.
- 7th day, add ½ cup (60 grams) rye flour and ¼ cup (60 ml) water; stir.

IF YOU ARE NOT READY to start the bread, refrigerate the starter until ready to use. Take it out of refrigerator the day before baking and let it to come to room temperature.

- 8th day, baking the bread.
- In a measuring cup with warm water, add sugar and yeast. Stir and let the yeast proof until foamy, 3-4 minutes.
- In the bowl of a stand mixer fitted with a dough hook, mix all dry ingredients: flour, garlic salt, Kosher salt, and all seeds.
- Add ¾ cup (200 grams) of starter and proof yeast.
- Blend mixture for 4 minutes on low - medium speed.
- Turn out dough onto a lightly floured work surface, form into a large ball, and place in a floured banneton basket or large greased bowl. Sprinkle the top with flour.
- Cover with a towel and let rise 30-60 minutes in a warm place. Meanwhile, preheat oven to 400° F (200° C).
- Once the dough is doubled in size, invert it onto a greased baking sheet or greased black iron pan (11"). Using scissors or a sharp knife, score the top with a cross shape (or a design of your choice). Brush the top with water.
- Bake for 30 minutes.

TIP *Your starter should weigh about 2–2 ½ cups (600 grams), add enough flour and water to bring it back to about 2 ½ cups (600 grams). It's always good to keep a little extra, because you will always lose a small amount.*

Carlsbad Crescents

Karlovarské Rohlíky

These crescents are made with sparkling natural mineral water. These were my favorite to eat when I was a little girl. The bakery that made the best Carlsbad Crescents was located by the bridge of Charles IV. I asked, "How come your crescents are so awesomely good?" The lady smiled and said, "Don't tell this to anyone—it is a secret. They are made with mineral water!" SHHH . . .

16 PIECES

1¼ cups (300 milliliters) mineral water

5 teaspoons (15 grams) active dry yeast

2 tablespoons (26 grams) sugar

4 cups (500 grams) all-purpose flour

7½ tablespoons (100 grams) unsalted butter, melted

3 teaspoons (9 grams) Diamond Crystal Kosher salt (If using another brand, begin with about half this amount and adjust to taste.)

- Warm up mineral water with sugar to 110° F (43° C), mix in dry yeast, stir, and let the yeast proof until foamy, 3-4 minutes.
- In the bowl of a stand mixer fitted with a dough hook, add flour, melted butter, salt, and risen yeast.
- Mix all ingredients together to form a dough.
- Cover the dough and allow it to rest for 30 minutes.
- Divide the dough into 4 even pieces, roll them into 4 balls, and let them rest for 10 minutes.
- Using a floured rolling pin, roll each ball into an 8-inch (20 cm) circle.
- Cut each circle into 4 wedges.
- By hand, stretch 3 corners so that the dough resembles a triangle with one short and two equally long sides.
- Starting at the short side, roll the dough up by hand.
- Turn the ends of roll toward each other to form a crescent.
- Cover and let rise for 30 minutes, or until doubled in size.
- Preheat oven to 400° F (200° C).
- Place crescents on a lightly greased baking sheet sprinkled with flour or lined with parchment paper.
- Brush with egg white.
- Bake for 12–15 minutes.

10
Kolaches
Koláče

Is it Czech or not?

Yes, Kolache is Czech! The name Kolache derives from Czech word *kolo*, meaning "wheel," which describes its shape. It came from the Moravia region of the Czech Republic.

It is the gem and pride of any Czech living in Texas, Nebraska, Oklahoma, or Wisconsin. People celebrate its birth and its heritage with festivals that draw visitors from all over the world.

People compete in contests for the honor of having the best kolaches. Every grandmother whose recipe was passed down to succeeding generations proudly created it like an artist, with love, passion, and joy. There exist as many recipes as grandmothers. They all differ from each other.

My recipe was passed down to me from my mother, and I converted it and tweaked it to American ingredients and understandings. As the creator of the most delicious kolaches in all of South Texas, I am devoted to my craft, which puts smiles on the faces of anyone who takes a bite of my delectable pastries.

Kolaches are a symbol of Czechs in the USA, and I am sharing my recipe with others to keep its beauty, taste, and pride alive.

Czech Kolaches

České Tradiční Koláče

My recipe is passed down from my mother and tweaked by me and my friends, Czech chefs (world award-winning pastry chef Lukaš Skála, who converted me to the pressing technique for kolaches) and others who helped me to match the authentic flavor. The traditional kolache is supposed to be round, dense, and golden brown!

24 PIECES

1⅓ cups (300 milliliters) milk, warm

1 teaspoon (4 grams) sugar

2 tablespoons (18 grams) active dry yeast

5 cups (600 grams) King Arthur unbleached all-purpose flour

½ cup (100 grams) sugar

1 whole egg

2 egg yolks

⅔ cup (150 grams) unsalted butter, melted

Zest of ½ lemon

2 teaspoons (6 grams) Diamond Crystal Kosher salt (If using another brand, start with half this amount and adjust to taste.

EGG WASH

2 egg yolks plus 1 tablespoon (15 milliliters) milk, whipped together

- Preheat oven to 350° F (175° C).
- Stir sugar with warm milk and then add yeast. Let the yeast proof until foamy.
- In the bowl of a stand mixer fitted with a paddle attachment, add flour, sugar, eggs, butter, lemon zest, and salt.
- Add risen yeast. Mix on low speed for 4 minutes, or until the dough is smooth. If the dough sticks to the sides of the bowl, use a spatula to scrape it down.
- Cover the bowl with plastic wrap and let the dough rise in a warm place until it doubles in size, about 30 minutes.
- Weigh 2 ounces (57 grams) of dough and shape it into a ball. Place each ball onto a cooking sheet lined with parchment paper. Make an indentation in the center of each ball with the floured bottom of a small glass to create a round disk.
- Brush the edges of the disk with egg wash and with wet fingers create a well, ready for filling.
- Put a spoonful of the filling you are using in each well.
- Top each filling with different toppings.
- Let kolaches rise again for 10 minutes.
- Bake for 18–20 minutes.

FILLINGS

Farmer's Cheese Kolaches are filled with Farmer's Cheese Filling (p. 143), topped with fruit of your choice, and sprinkled with streusels (p. 144) or powdered sugar.

Plum Jam Kolaches are filled with fresh Plum Jam (p. 140) and sprinkled with streusels.

Poppy Seed Kolaches are filled with Poppy Seed Paste (p. 141) and sprinkled with slivers of almonds. Don't sprinkle powdered sugar on Plum Jam or Poppy Seed Kolaches.

Plum Jam Paste

Povidlová Nápln

Plum jam is made out of sugar plums, known in the US as Italian plums, boiled and then rubbed through a sieve. With the evaporation of water, the jam becomes concentrated. Plum jam, in comparison to marmalades, is prepared with very small amounts of sugar.

In my recipe, we use dry sugar plums (prunes) because they are easier to find.

The word *povidla* has been documented in Czechia since the 14th century (Klaret's dictionary) and has been adopted by other languages such as Polish, Ukrainian, Austrian, and German. So you can use the name *Povidla* in English too.

MAKES 50 OUNCES

1 pound (450 grams) prunes

2 tablespoons sugar, or to taste

Zest of 1 medium-size orange

1 cup (240 milliliters) fresh-squeezed orange juice

Zest of 1 lemon

½ cup (120 milliliters) fresh-squeezed lemon juice

2 teaspoons (5 grams) ground cinnamon

½ teaspoon ground cloves

- Carefully slice all the prunes to make sure that there are not any pits.
- Soak sliced prunes in the fresh-squeezed orange and lemon juices overnight.
- Grind prunes in a meat grinder. Save the juices for next step.
- Using an immersion blender, mix ground prunes and juices with zest from orange and lemon, cinnamon, cloves, and sugar.

STORE the plum paste in the refrigerator.

TIP *Plum jam is used as a filling for pastries or dumplings and as a sweet spread on bread or toast.*

Poppy Seed Paste

Maková nádivka

Did you know that the Czech Republic holds the poppy power? Yes, the Czechs are the top producers of poppy seeds, by far.

You have to know that there are two kinds of poppies. The one that is harvested immaturely has undeveloped poppy pods with milky sap extract that is turned into opium. The other one, which is harvested in the Czech Republic, is grown for food. It has no narcotic properties. The poppy grows until the poppy capsule dries up and the capsule looks like wood. On the inside of this capsule are loose poppy seeds, and when you shake the capsule, the seeds make a sound like rain. In this stage, the seeds on the inside are ready to come out and be used for cooking! This poppy seed paste recipe is used for filling kolaches and other baked goods.

MAKES 30 OUNCES

2 cups (250 grams) poppy seeds, ground

2½ cups (600 milliliters) milk

½ cup (100 grams) sugar

Peel of ½ lemon

1 tablespoon current jelly or apricot jam

- Grind poppy seeds in a nut or coffee grinder.
- In a pot, bring milk, ground poppy seeds, sugar, and lemon peel to a boil, and then immediately reduce the heat to a very low simmer.
- Stir frequently until the milk is evaporated and thick paste is created, about 45 minutes.
- Discard lemon peel, mix in jelly, and let cool.

TIP

- *Ninja mixer does a great job for all nut grinding. Grind only as much as you need.*
- *If the poppy seed mixture puffs hard as it comes to a boil, pull the pot from the heat to cool, then replace and continue to cook on a low simmer.*
- *Fresh poppy seeds have very distinctive taste. They can get rancid quickly if not stored properly. Once poppy seeds smell rancid they also taste bitter. To keep poppy seeds fresh, store in a sealed glass jar in dry, dark, cool place, where they will stay fresh for up to 6 months.*

Applesauce

Jablečné Pyre

As a little girl, I would go to a store called Ovoce-Zelenina (produce store) and buy a frozen apple puree and eat it as an ice cream.

Apple puree will enrich many different desserts. I like to use it for making kolaches.

7 Granny apples, peeled, cored and diced

1½ cups Chardonnay wine

5 whole cloves

¾ cup (150 grams) brown sugar

- In a pot, simmer apples, wine and cloves for 20 minutes.
- When apples are cooked, add sugar and blend the mixture with an immersion blender.

SERVE with potato pancakes or use this puree as a filling for Kolaches.

TIP *You can substitute apples for pears.*

Farmer's Cheese Filling

Tvarohová Nápln

Quark, cottage cheese, fromage blanc, farmer's cheese, and queso fresco are all made from curds of acidified milk. The whey, which is separated from the curds, is used for making ricotta cheese. In my experience, the best fresh cheese for making kolaches is ricotta cheese, which can be substituted for farmer's cheese, which is hard to find in stores.

1½ cups (350 grams) ricotta cheese (If ricotta is watery, let it drain overnight in a fine mesh strainer.)

1 cup (250 grams) cream cheese

1 egg yolk

3 tablespoons (40 grams) sugar

1½ tablespoons (20 grams) 1 package Dr. Oetker of vanilla sugar

Zest of ½ lemon

IN THE BOWL of a stand mixer fitted with a paddle attachment, mix all ingredients together.

TIP *You can use a food processor instead of a mixer. The cheese filling will be firmer.*

Streusel

Drobenka, Posypka, a Žmolenka

These sweet crumbs are delicious on desserts full of juicy fruits because they soak up the juices and add an extra layer of butter. Each of the three Czech regions has its own name for "Streusel." The three names listed below come from verbs which describe an action making this topping.

Drobenka comes from verb *drobit* – "to crumble."

Posypka comes from verb *sypat* – "to pour."

Žmolenka comes from verb *žmoulat* – "to break the butter with fingers together with sugar and flour."

7½ teaspoons (100 grams) unsalted butter

1 cup plus 1 tablespoon (150 grams) all-purpose flour

¾ cup (150 grams) sugar

1 package of vanilla sugar

- Crumble all the ingredients together with your fingers.
- Sprinkle on top of kolaches or other pastries.
- Store in a container in refrigerator.

Wedding Kolaches Tradition

Svatebni Tradice

There are two superstitions: One superstition says that the bride herself should avoid baking so as not to have crying children. The other superstition says that a bride should be participating in baking to prove to the groom that she is worthy of marriage.

Tradition dictates that future newlyweds should personally distribute kolaches to family, friends, and neighbors. Wedding Kolaches should have at least three different fillings. They are baked about two to three weeks before the wedding. The round Wedding Kolaches represent money, and young newlyweds hope for a dollar for each kolache to collect and save to get a good start. One thousand kolaches, representing $1,000, is the typical goal. There are also Corner Kolaches (in this book, we call them Four-Corner Kolaches), which in some regions are tasted by bridesmaids who want to get married.

Wedding Kolaches

Svatební Koláčky

Wedding Kolaches are served at nearly every wedding reception in the Czech Republic. They make appearances at many different celebrations too. These tiny kolaches are great for any occasion when many people gather together.

They are fast and easy!

39 PIECES

½ cup plus 2 tablespoons (130 grams) milk

1 teaspoon (4 grams) sugar

2 teaspoons (6 grams) active dry yeast

1 cup plus 2 tablespoons (250 grams) unsalted butter, room temperature

1 egg

4 tablespoons (30 grams) confectioner sugar

Pinch of Diamond Crystal Kosher salt

2 cups plus 2 tablespoons (300 grams) all-purpose flour, sifted

4 tablespoons (30 grams) sifted confectioner sugar, for dipping

1 package of vanilla sugar, for dipping

EGG WASH

2 egg yolks plus 1 tablespoon (15 milliliters) milk, beaten together.

- Stir sugar with warm milk, and then add yeast. Let the yeast proof until foamy.
- In the bowl of a stand mixer with a whisk attachment, whisk butter, egg, salt, and sugar until fluffy.
- Add flour and proofed yeast to the butter mixture.
- Change the whisk attachment to a flat paddle attachment. Mix it on low speed until very smooth. Scrap dough down from sides of bowl. Do not let the dough rise.
- Transfer the dough to a heavily floured work surface and gently roll out four loaves.
- Let the loaves rest in the refrigerator for 30 minutes.
- Preheat oven to 375° F (190° C).
- Cut 0.7 ounces (28 grams) of dough for small balls.
- Roll them heavily in flour before placing them on a buttered baking sheet.
- Press down each ball with your floured palm to flatten them.
- Make an indentation with your finger in the center of each disk.
- Brush the edges with egg wash.
- Place farmer's cheese or plum jam filling in the center and sprinkle with streusel, or use poppyseed paste and top with almonds.
- Bake for 12–15 minutes.
- Roll in powder sugar.

Four-Corner Kolaches

Šátečkové Koláčky

The exact translation for these kolaches would be "Scarf Kolaches" because they are folded by the corners, like folding a scarf. I did not like the translation, so I changed the name in English to Four-Corner Kolaches, as the technique for folding describes.

12 PIECES

1¼ cups (150 grams) all-purpose flour, sifted

¼ cup (50 grams) sugar, sifted

¾ cup (175 grams) ricotta cheese

7½ tablespoons (100 grams) unsalted butter, room temperature

Pinch of Diamond Crystal Kosher salt

Zest of ½ lemon

¾ cup (200 grams) of any filling—farmer's cheese, poppy seed, or plum jam

3 ounces (80 grams) sliced almonds

EGG WASH

2 egg yolks plus 1 tablespoon (15 milliliters) milk, beaten together.

- Preheat oven to 375° F (190° C).
- In the bowl of a stand mixer fitted with a dough hook, blend flour, sugar, ricotta cheese, butter, salt, and lemon zest.
- Roll out the dough to 9 x 12 inches (23 cm x 30 cm) and cut 3-inch (7.5 cm) squares. Roll each of these into a 4-inch (10 cm) square.
- Place filling in the center and bring the corners to the middle. With your fingers pinch three corners together above the filling, and then carefully press the fourth corner so that the filling will not pop out of the kolache.
- Brush kolaches with egg wash and sprinkle with sliced almonds.
- Bake for 20 minutes, or until they are golden brown.

SERVE sprinkled with powder sugar and enjoy as a little snack at any time.

Sugar Plum Square Kolaches

Švestkový Kolač

Švestkový Kolač is sometimes translated as "Plum Cake" because the dough is rolled onto a baking sheet instead of shaping it into smaller pastries. Kolaches are an appropriate name, though, because the ingredients vary very little. A Square Kolache is faster to make, and you can fill it up with more fruit. A kolache baked on a baking sheet was my mother's favorite. She felt less guilty eating it because it had more fruit than dough.

12 SERVINGS

4 cups (500 grams) all-purpose flour

⅓ cup (67 grams) sugar

Pinch of Diamond Crystal Kosher salt

½ cup plus 1 tablespoon (125 grams) unsalted butter

2 egg yolks

1 teaspoon (4 grams) vanilla extract

1 cup (250 milliliters) milk

1 teaspoon (4 grams) sugar

2 tablespoons (18 grams) active dry yeast

4 pounds (1,800 grams) fresh sugar plums, also known as Italian plums, pitted

Cinnamon, sugar, and streusel for topping

EGG WASH

2 egg yolks beaten together with 1 tablespoon (15 milliliters) milk

- Preheat oven to 375° F (190° C).
- Stir sugar into warm milk and then add yeast. Let the yeast proof until foamy.
- In the bowl of a stand mixer fitted with a paddle attachment, add sifted flour, sugar, salt, butter, yolks, and vanilla extract.
- Add proofed yeast. Mix all ingredients on low speed for 1 minute, then increase the speed and mix for 4 minutes until the dough is smooth. If the dough sticks to the sides of the bowl, scrape down with a spatula.
- Cover the bowl with plastic wrap and let the dough rise in a warm place until it doubles in size.
- Grease and flour your baking pan.
- On a floured table, roll out a rectangle as big as your pan and transfer the dough to the pan.
- If the dough is little bigger than the pan, cut the edges off and roll them into a long string. Place this string around the perimeter of the kolache and press the inner half into flat dough.
- Brush the edge with egg wash, then gently prick the dough with a fork to allow steam to escape during baking.
- With a spatula, spread the farmer's cheese over the dough, then place sugar plums on top.
- Sprinkle with cinnamon, sugar, and streusel.
- Bake for 45 minutes.

SERVE with powdered sugar and Chantilly cream.

CHANTILLY CREAM

1 cup (250 milliliters) 33% or more butterfat heavy cream and 4 tablespoons (30 grams) powdered sugar, whipped together.

TIP *Sugar plums are known in the United States as Italian plums and are harvested in August.*

You can use blueberries or apricots instead of sugar plums. Everyone one will love them!

Family-Style Kolache

Frgál

The *Frgál*, or "pie" kolache, is a unique and centuries-old Wallachian dessert. Every slice gives distinct flavors to be relished with each bite. It originated in the late 1800s in the easternmost mountain Moravian region of the Czech Republic and featured sauerkraut or beet filling.

Round like a large pizza, these desserts are sweet and have been adapted to come in a variety of fruit fillings. The test of a perfect Frgál is the dough, which must rise three times: first immediately after the dough is made, second after it's been divided into individual bowls, and finally right before it is put in the oven. This process ensures proper tenderness of the pie.

Traditionally, Frgáls are made for weddings and holiday celebrations. Its unique taste is quite sensational as its appearance is beautifully decorated in rich fruit flavors and colors. As a tribute to its enduring popularity, the Frgál is known as a unique bakery product—a delicacy. In fact, it became protected with a geographical indication in 2013 in the Czech Republic.

12 SERVINGS

1 cup (250 milliliters) milk

1 teaspoon (4 grams) sugar, for the yeast to proof

4 tablespoons (36 grams) active dry yeast

6 cups (750 grams) Wondra flour, sifted

2 cups (250 grams) all-purpose flour, sifted

2 teaspoons (6 grams) Diamond Crystal Kosher salt (If using another brand, start with half this amount and adjust to taste.)

Pinch of nutmeg

1 lemon zest

1 cup plus 2 tablespoons (250 grams) unsalted butter

½ cup plus 2 tablespoons (125 grams) sugar

1 teaspoon (4 grams) vanilla extract

1 tablespoon (15 milliliters) rum

6 whole eggs plus one egg for egg wash

1 cup (250 milliliters) heavy cream, warm

- Preheat oven to 375° F (190° C).
- Stir sugar with warm milk and then add yeast. Let the yeast proof until foamy.
- In the bowl of a stand mixer fitted with a dough hook, add sifted Wondra and all-purpose flour, salt, nutmeg, and zest.
- On the side, cream butter, sugar, vanilla, and rum.
- Add butter mixture and eggs to flour mixture.
- Add risen yeast and heavy cream to the mixture and work into a dough on low speed 2 for 1 minute and then increase the speed to 4 and mix for 4 minutes until the dough is smooth. If the dough sticks to the sides of the bowl, use a spatula to scrape it down.

- Sprinkle the dough with flour and cover with plastic wrap. Let it rise.

- On a floured table, divide the dough into 4 equal parts about 550 grams each and roll each piece into ball. Let balls rise.
- Roll each ball into a 16-inch circle.
- Place the Frgál on a baking sheet and fold outer edge toward the center. Create a half inch edge.
- Press the end of the edge with your fingers down to the main Frgál.
- Brush the edges with an egg wash made from 2 egg yolks and 1 tablespoon (15 milliliters) milk. Then, using your finger, create a well along the edge.
- Poke holes with a wooden stick into the bottom of the Frgál.
- Place a filling of your choice into the middle of the Frgál. It should always have farmer's cheese on the bottom and fruit paste on the top.
- Sprinkle with streusel.
- Bake in the oven for 20 minutes.

SERVE: Cut it into pizza size wedges and enjoy.

TIP *You can be very creative here. Use all different fillings. Place the filling into the piping pastry bag and go wild! The easiest Frgál with different fillings I call "Fiesta." Pipe in the circles of different flavors and dress them up with almonds, raisins, chocolate chips. You will get different flavors in every bite.*

Moravian Kolaches

Dvojctihodé Koláče

The Czechs call these kolaches Moravian Kolaches because they come from Moravia, but Moravians call these same kolaches "venerable."

Moravian Kolaches are filled with two fillings—usually on the inside with farmer's cheese, then topped with plum jam. My children always preferred fresh strawberries on the top. You can choose your own toppings.

16 KOLACHES

1 cup (250 milliliters) milk, warm

1 teaspoon (4 grams) sugar

2 tablespoons (18 grams) active dry yeast

2¾ cups (350 grams) all-purpose flour

1 cup plus 1 tablespoon (150 grams) Wondra flour

⅜ cup (90 grams) sugar

2 teaspoons (6 grams) Diamond Crystal Kosher salt (If using another brand, start with half this amount and adjust to taste.)

1 whole egg

2 egg yolks

½ cup plus 2 tablespoons (120 grams) vegetable oil

Zest of ½ lemon

1½ tablespoons (20 grams) 1 package Dr. Oetker of vanilla sugar

1 pound (450 grams) fresh strawberries, or any fruit filling like plum jam

Streusel, for topping kolaches

1 pound (450 grams) Farmer's Cheese Filling

(continues)

EGG WASH

2 egg yolks and 1 tablespoon (15 milliliters) milk, beaten together

- Preheat oven to 350° F (175° C).
- Stir sugar with warm milk and then add yeast. Let the yeast proof until foamy.
- In the bowl of a stand mixer fitted with a dough hook add flours, sugar, salt, eggs, oil, lemon zest, and vanilla sugar.
- Add proofed yeast. Mix all ingredients on low speed 1 minute, then increase the speed and mix for 4 minutes until the dough is smooth. If the dough sticks to the sides of the bowl, scrape down with a spatula.
- Cover the bowl with plastic wrap and let rise in a warm place until it doubles in size.
- Divide the dough into 2.5 ounce (57 grams) balls. Let rise for 30 minutes.
- Roll the dough into 7-inch (18 cm) circles, and place in the center a dollop of farmer's cheese filling. Bring the sides of the circle toward the center and close the farmer's cheese inside. Make sure that there are no seams where the cheese could escape. Keep your fingers dry.
- Let rise for 30 minutes.
- Press down on the ball carefully to create a 6 inch disk. In the center of the disk, make an indentation.
- Brush the edges of the disk with egg wash and with wet fingers gently create a well, ready for fruit filling or fresh fruit.
- Fill with your favorite fruit filling. I like strawberries.
- Sprinkle the strawberries with streusel and bake kolaches in the oven for 20 minutes.

TIP *This dough needs to rise very well so that it will be easier to stretch with your fingers to 6-inch circles.*

11

Sweet Favorites

Nejoblíbenější Sladkasti

Life is sweet in the Czech Republic!

The excellent success of the Prague masters of confectioners like Frantisek Myšák (my mother's friend), Antonín Berger, and others influenced many followers in various cities of the Republic and significantly raised the level of the confectionery profession in Czechoslovakia.

When all private businesses were nationalized and everyone had to go to work, all women took a job in factories with sweets. They didn't have time anymore for baking at home and had to purchase sweets for the family. This created a large volume of sales, and the Czech confectionary bloomed.

Czechs love their sweets from canapes to pralines, cream rolls, or imaginatively shaped cakes that can be swallowed by the eyes in addition to the mouth.

Today confectionery stores make desserts right in front of you, so it's hard to resist and not get one of each. The confectionery stores continue the tradition of the First Republic and bake without preservatives and substitutes. Everything is fresh!

With my recipes you can continue this tradition for your family and create mouthwatering desserts.

Cherry Coffee Cake

Třený Koláč s Ovocem (Bublanina)

The name *Bublanina* derives from the Czech word *bublat* (bubbling), because baking fruit in a cake gives the impression that the dessert is bubbling.

8 SERVINGS

1¼ cups plus 2 tablespoons (300 grams) unsalted butter, room temperature

1½ cups (300 grams) sugar

5 eggs, separated

1¾ cups plus 2 tablespoons (300 grams) Wondra flour

2 teaspoons (10 grams) butter for spring form

1 tablespoon (10 grams) flour for dusting the spring form

2 cups (280 grams) sour cherries

2 tablespoons (16 grams) flour for coating cherries

½ cup (60 grams) streusel

½ cup (60 grams) sliced almonds

- Preheat oven to 350° F (175° C).
- In the bowl of a stand mixer fitted with a wire whip attachment, mix butter, sugar and yolks until the batter is fluffy. About 10 minutes.
- Grease the spring form and dust with flour.
- On the side, whip the egg whites to a peak with hand mixer.
- On very slow speed, alternate adding whipped egg whites and flour spoon by spoon.
- Pour the cake batter into a spring form, add sour cherries rolled in flour, and sprinkle with streusel. Sprinkle sliced almonds and place it in the oven.
- Bake for 45 minutes.

SERVE with powder sugar and Chantilly Cream.

TIP *Replace sour cherries with different fresh fruit like blueberries, strawberries, or even bananas.*

Bavarian Doughnuts

Bavorské Vdolky

My grandmother was the best donut baker! Even though I never met her, I cherish her recipes and keep the tradition going.

24 PIECES

¾ cup (190 milliliters) milk, warm

1 teaspoon (4 grams) sugar

1½ tablespoons (13 grams) active dry yeast

7½ tablespoons (100 grams) unsalted butter

¼ cup (50 grams) sugar

1 teaspoon (3 grams) of Diamond Crystal Kosher salt (If using another brand, start with half this amount and adjust to taste.)

3 egg yolks

½ of lemon zest

3¼ cups (400 grams) all-purpose flour

1 pound (450 grams) and 4 cups (1 liter) canola oil, for frying

- Stir sugar with warm milk and then add yeast. Let the yeast proof until foamy.
- In the bowl of a stand mixer fitted with a wire whip attachment, whip butter, sugar and salt.
- Add egg yolks and zest.
- Add flour and proof yeast.
- Work a smooth dough, cover with plastic wrap and let it rise for 30 minutes in a warm place.
- Roll the dough about ¾ inch high (2 cm). With 3 inch (7.5 cm) circle cookie cutter, cut donuts. Let them rise for 30 minutes. Press the center of the donut with a small circumference cup or glass to make an indentation.
- Heat up half of the butter/oil combination. To know when the temperature of the oil is perfect, throw a piece of bread into oil, and when it bubbles around the bread, the oil is ready for frying. Don't let the oil bubble too hard.
- Fry risen donuts covered with a lid for 2 minutes. Flip them over and fry them without the lid for 2 more minutes or until they are golden brown.

SERVE with Plum Jam and Chantilly cream.

Czech Braided Christmas Bread Tradition

Vánočka

In the spirit of the religious tradition, the leavening of the dough represented the rising of wealth and abundance. It was very important that the dough would rise evenly, without falling down. For that reason women helped the process of dough rising high by jumping up. If the Vánočka cracked, it was an unfortunate and failed year. Therefore, the women did not say a word during its preparation and focused only on work.

There is lot of symbolism in the shape of Vánočka. There are three layers of braided dough. The bottom one is made out of four-strand braids which represent earth, sun, water, and air. The second layer consists of three strands that represent wisdom, will, and sense. The top layer is made only with two strands that stand for knowledge and love. True or not, I like this version of the legend.

In the earlier times, individual Vánočka were baked for all members of the family. The largest one was placed on the table and cut by the housekeeper. He gave a piece of bread to the animals to protect them from evil forces, and threw the crumbs into a well to keep them from drying out. The remains were left to souls of the dead, who reportedly visit the homes of their living loved ones on Christmas Eve.

Czech Braided Christmas Bread

Vánočka

Vánočka is a symbol of the Czech Christmas. Baking Vánočka is one of the oldest Christmas customs that have survived to this day. Its shape is supposed to resemble baby Jesus wrapped in a blanket. If you are going to prepare the Vánočka this year at your home, don't forget to bake a coin into it. He who finds the coin in his slice, health and wealth awaits him in the following year.

1 LOAF

1 cup (250 ml) milk, warm

1 teaspoon (4 grams) sugar

2 tablespoons (18 grams) active dry yeast

3¼ cups (400 grams) all-purpose flour

⅓ cup plus 3 teaspoons (80 grams) sugar

2 egg yolks

7½ tablespoons (100 grams) butter, room temperature

½ of lemon zest

Pinch of Diamond Crystal Kosher salt

½ cup (60 grams) black raisins

¾ cup (80 grams) sliced almonds

EGG WASH

2 egg yolks beaten together with 1 tablespoon (15 milliliters) milk

- Preheat oven to 350° F (175° C).
- Stir sugar with warm milk and then add yeast. Let the yeast proof until foamy.
- In the bowl of a stand mixer fitted with a dough hook, add flour, sugar, eggs, butter, lemon zest, and salt.
- Add risen yeast. Mix it on low speed 2 for 4 minutes until the dough is smooth. If the dough sticks to the sides of the bowl, use a spatula to scrape it down.
- Cover the bowl with plastic wrap, and let the dough rise in a warm place until it doubles in size. About 30 minutes.
- Divide the dough into 9 equal pieces and roll it into balls. Let them rest for 10 minutes and roll each ball into 14 inch (36 cm) long logs. As you work with them, they will shrink into a 12-inch (30 cm) long logs.
- First braid 4 pieces. Outside log over next two, one direction and repeat from the other side, outside log over next two. Pinch the ends tightly.
- Press the center of this braid down to form a space for next layer.
- Braid 3 pieces. One over the other from the right side and then one over the other from the left side. Pinch the ends tightly.
- Press the center of this braid down to form a space for the next layer.
- Braid two pieces together, one over the other, and place it in the well of the second layer.
- Let the bread rest for 20 minutes.
- Brush the bread with egg wash and sprinkle with almonds.
- Insert toothpicks through the braided layers to keep them from falling.
- Bake in the oven for 30 minutes.

SERVE with coffee, milk, or tea.

TIP *If the bread gets old, dip slices of bread in cinnamon-egg-milk mixture and fry until golden brown to make French toast. Sprinkle with powdered sugar.*

Leavened Strawberry Dumpling

Jahodový Kynutý Knedlík

When you say, "The way to a person's heart is through the stomach," that applies to this special dish. All you have to do is sprinkle dumplings with freshly made fried bread crumbs, cinnamon sugar, and melted butter! Mmm, simply yummy!

9 DUMPLINGS

1½ cups (350 milliliters) milk, warm

1 tablespoon (13 grams) sugar

5 teaspoons (15 grams) active dry yeast

3½ cups (500 grams) Wondra flour or hard red wheat flour

1 egg

2 teaspoons (6 grams) Diamond Crystal Kosher salt (If using another brand, start with half this amount and adjust to taste.)

1 pound (454 grams) strawberries

FOR COOKING DUMPLINGS use a steamer basket that is inserted into a pot with boiling water. The water must not touch the bottom of the basket.

- Stir sugar with warm milk and then add yeast. Let the yeast proof until foamy.
- In the bowl of a stand mixer fitted with a paddle attachment, add flour, sugar, eggs, and salt.
- Add risen yeast. Mix it on slow speed for 4 minutes until the dough is smooth. If the dough sticks to the sides of the bowl, use a spatula to scrape it down.
- Remove the dough out of the mixing bowl on lightly floured surface. Divide the dough into nine 3½ ounces (100 grams) balls. Cover them and let them rise.
- Flatten risen balls and place strawberries in the center. Bring the sides up to cover the strawberries. Pinch the seam so that strawberries stay secured inside.
- Set each dumpling with its seam side down, cover with a towel, and let it rest for 10 minutes.
- Bring water in pot to boil.
- When water is boiling, place 3 dumplings into the steamer basket lined with a clean kitchen towel, and steam them covered with a lid for 10 minutes.
- Before you take the dumplings out of the steamer basket, pull one out and check for doneness by cutting it in the middle using a sewing thread. If you see that the dough is still raw on the inside, replace in the steamer basket for additional 2–4 minutes. Check the time when all the dumplings are done, and adjust cooking time accordingly.
- Repeat for the rest of dumplings. Don't forget to refill water and bring to boil.
- Once they are out of the water, poke a hole with a fork to let the steam out and so that dumplings stay nice and round.

SERVE with fried bread crumbs, sprinkled with cinnamon-sugar mix, and topped with melted butter.

Chantilly Cream Pound Cake

Šlehačková Bábovka

A simple recipe with a great result: this moist and good looking creamy cake. Like other cake recipes, you can customize this one. Add cocoa powder, chocolate, lemon peel, or chopped nuts to the cake.

12-16 SERVINGS

6 whole eggs

½ cup (50 grams) sugar

2 cups plus 4 tablespoons (500 milliliters) heavy cream

3½ cups (500 grams) all-purpose flour

2 packets vanilla sugar

½ lemon zest

2 teaspoons (8 grams) baking powder

1 teaspoon (3 grams) Diamond Crystal Kosher salt (If using another brand, start with half this amount and adjust to taste.)

1 tablespoon (14 grams) butter for the form

½ cup (50 grams) bread crumbs

- Preheat oven to 400° F (200° C).
- In the bowl of a stand mixer fitted with a wire whip attachment, mix first 8 ingredients together.
- Grease the form for pound cake with butter and dust with bread crumbs.
- Pour the cake batter into the form and place it in the oven.
- Bake for 45 minutes.

SERVE with powder sugar.

TIP *For poppy seed pound cake pour only half of the batter into the form. Add poppy seed paste, and then cover it with the other half of the batter.*

For chocolate marble pound cake, save 1/3 of the batter, add cocoa powder, and mix it well. Spread the chocolate mixture on half of the batter, and cover it with the rest of the batter.

Sugar Plum Dumplings

Švestkové Knedlíky

Using fresh and in-season ingredients is one of the things that is so beautiful about the Czech cuisine. So, for example, in April you will make strawberry dumplings because they are in season. In May you will make apricot and peach dumplings and kolaches, and then in July and August you will make sugar plum dumplings and kolaches.

12 DUMPLINGS

2.2 pounds (1,000 grams) Yukon golden potatoes, cooked with skin on

4 teaspoons (12 grams) Diamond Crystal Kosher salt (If using another brand, start with half this amount and adjust to taste).

2 whole eggs

1¾ cups (225 grams) Wondra or hard red wheat flour

½ cup (75 grams) semolina flour

1 pound (450 grams) fresh sugar plums (also known as Italian plums), pitted

¼ cup (60 grams) unsalted butter, for brushing tops of dumplings

Powder sugar, ground poppy seeds, and melted butter for topping

FOR COOKING DUMPLINGS use a steamer basket that is inserted into a pot with boiling water. The water must not touch the bottom of the basket.

- Place washed raw potatoes in the pot and cover them with cold water. Cook them until they are al dente, still a little firm, for about 30–35 minutes.
- Let potatoes cool.
- Peel cooked potatoes and grate them on a fine grater into a mixing bowl.
- Add salt, eggs, and flours. With your hands, first blend all ingredients in a bowl, and then finish by kneading into a smooth dough on a floured surface.
- Roll the dough about ½ inch (1.5 cm) thick and cut into 3 inch (7.5 cm) x 3 inch (7.5 cm) squares.
- Place a sugar plum in the center of the square, and bring the sides toward the center to wrap the fruit. Roll the dumpling, making sure that you don't leave any open seams.
- Have a steamer basket with boiling water ready.
- When water is boiling, place four dumplings into the steamer basket lined with a clean kitchen towel and steam them, covered with a lid, for 10–15 minutes.
- Before you take the dumplings out of the steamer basket, pull one out and check for doneness by cutting it in the middle using a sewing thread. If the dough is still raw in the middle, replace in the steamer basket for an additional 2–4 minutes. Check the time when the dumplings are done, and adjust cooking time accordingly.
- Remove cooked dumplings from the basket with a fork. Poke holes through the top of each dumpling to release steam. Brush them with melted butter.
- Repeat with the rest of dumplings.

SERVE with a mixture of ground poppy seeds and powder sugar topped with melted butter.

Fried Bread Crumbs

Smažená Strouhanka

Sprinkle these bread crumbs over your dumplings and when you add melted butter, oh yes, that is paradise!

4-6 SERVINGS

7 ounces (200 grams) unsalted butter, melted

3 cups plus 3 tablespoons (300 grams) bread crumbs

⅓ cup (85 grams) brown sugar

- In a sauté pan, fry bread crumbs in butter on low heat until they are golden brown. Stir occasionally.
- Add sugar once the bread crumbs are cool.

Reverse Apricot (Fruit) Dumplings

Something new, something vogue! Instead of the fruit being inside of dumplings, the fruit is cooked on the side. This recipe will put a smile on everyone's face.

4-6 SERVINGS

2 cups whole-milk ricotta cheese (500 grams) drained

1¼ cups (200 grams) Wondra flour or hard red wheat flour

¼ cup (50 grams) semolina flour

2 whole eggs

⅓ cup (40 grams) sugar

1 teaspoon (3 grams) Diamond Crystal Kosher salt (If using another brand, start with half this amount and adjust to taste.)

¼ cup (60 grams) vegetable oil or melted butter

7–14 apricots, washed, pitted

6 quarts of water for boiling the dumplings

1 teaspoon (3 grams) Diamond Crystal Kosher salt, for boiling water (If using another brand, start with half this amount and adjust to taste.)

Cinnamon-sugar mixture, for serving

1 cup (120 grams) unsalted butter, melted, for topping

SEASONAL FRUIT SAUCE

⅓ cup (60 grams) vegetable oil, for coating dumplings

1 pound (450 grams) apricots, pitted

½ pound (230 grams) blueberries or any other fruit

¼ cup (60 grams) unsalted butter

½ teaspoon (2 grams) cinnamon

Juice of ½ lemon

Sugar to taste

- In a large bowl, combine both flours, sugar, salt, ricotta cheese, eggs, and oil. Using your hands, combine ingredients to form a smooth dough. Do not overwork the dough!
- On a lightly floured surface, form two cylindrical loaves, each 2 inches (5cm) high. Let loaves rest, covered, for 20 minutes.
- In a large pot, bring water with salt to a boil.
- Form small dumplings, about one heaping tablespoon or 1.2–1.3 ounces (35 grams).
- Reduce the boiling water to medium heat and carefully drop in dumplings.
- Immediately stir the dumplings so that they do not stick to the bottom of the pot.
- Cook for 8–10 minutes. Remove one dumpling, and with a thread, cut through the middle to see if it is cooked. If not, replace the halves and cook for a couple more minutes.
- Make a note of the total time so you will know how long to cook the next batch.
- Using a slotted spoon, transfer dumplings into a bowl with oil and roll them. Remove dumplings and keep them covered to stay warm.
- Meanwhile, melt butter in a skillet over low heat. Add sugar and cinnamon. Stir to melt sugar. Add fruit and cook for 4–5 minutes. Add lemon juice.

TO SERVE: Spoon cooked fruit with sauce around and over dumplings. Top with Chantilly cream and fresh mint.

CHANTILLY CREAM:

1 cup (240 ml) heavy cream

2 tablespoons (28 grams) powdered sugar

Fresh mint

WHIP heavy cream and sugar until it forms peaks.

Ricotta Cheese Apricot Dumplings

Merunkové Knedlíky (Tvarohové)

Do you feel guilty about eating dumplings? Fruit dumplings are perhaps the most popular sweet food in Czechia. Everybody loves the taste, and adding cheese to the dough should make you less guilty about eating too much dough.

10 DUMPLINGS

2 cups whole-milk ricotta cheese (500 grams), drained

1¼ cups (200 grams) Wondra flour or hard red wheat flour

¼ cup (50 grams) semolina flour

2 whole eggs

⅓ cup (67 grams) sugar

1 teaspoon (3 grams) Diamond Crystal Kosher salt (If using another brand, start with half this amount and adjust to taste.)

¼ cup (60 grams) oil or melted butter

7–14 apricots, washed, pitted

6 quarts of water for boiling the dumplings

1 teaspoon (3 grams) Diamond Crystal Kosher salt, for boiling water (If using another brand, start with half this amount and adjust to taste.)

Cinnamon-sugar mixture, for serving

1 cup (120 grams) unsalted butter, melted, for topping

- In a large bowl, combine both flours, sugar, salt, ricotta cheese, eggs, and oil. Using your hands, combine ingredients to form a smooth dough. Do not overwork the dough!
- On a lightly floured surface, form two cylindrical loaves, each 2 inches (5 cm) high. Let loaves rest, covered, for 20 minutes.
- In a large pot, bring water with salt to boil.
- Slice each loaf into 5 pieces and place the apricot in the middle of each circle.
- Wrap the apricot with the dough, making sure that you don't have any open seams.
- Reduce the boiling water to medium heat and carefully drop in dumplings. Immediately stir the dumplings so that they do not stick to the bottom of the pot.
- Cook for 8–10 minutes. Half way through, turn the dumplings over. Once they come up to the surface, they should be done. Remove one dumpling, and with a thread, cut through the middle to see if it is cooked. If not, place dumpling back and cook for couple more minutes.
- Make a note of the total time so you will know how long to cook the remaining dumplings.
- Remove cooked dumplings from basket, and with a fork poke holes through the top of the dumplings to release steam.
- Roll dumplings in fried bread crumbs, sprinkle with cinnamon-sugar mix, and top with melted butter.

FRIED BREAD CRUMBS

1 cup (200 grams) unsalted butter, melted

3 cups plus 3 tablespoons (300grams) bread crumbs

½ cup (85 grams) brown sugar

- In a sauté pan, fry bread crumbs in butter on low heat until golden brown. Stir occasionally. Add sugar once the bread crumbs are cool.

Palatschinken

Palačinky

The difference between Palatschinken and French crêpes is that French crêpes are made from thin batter and are folded into quarters, and Palatschinken are made with thicker batter, filled with jam, rolled, and sprinkled with powder sugar or topped with Chantilly cream.

As the story goes, the Hungarian Count Esterhazy's chef, Francisco Palaccini, who was born in Rumania, stole the idea at a banquet in Paris in the 17th century and put a spin on it.

Now there is a fight between Hungarians and Romanians claiming the origins of Palatschinken. But it was the Czechs who started to call it *Palačinka,* and from that the Austrians and Germans started to call it *Palatschinke*. So is it Hungarian, Romanian, or Czech? I will go with the Czech, because most of the names of sweet dishes derive from the Czech language. On the other hand, most of the names of savory dishes derive from the German language.

4-6 SERVINGS

1½ cups plus 2 tablespoons (200 grams) all-purpose flour

2 eggs

1¾ cups (400 milliliters) milk

Pinch of Diamond Crystal Kosher salt

Butter for sautéing

- In a mixer, blend flour, eggs, milk, and salt.
- In a nonstick skillet with butter, cook one ladle of Palatschiken batter for 4 minutes on one side, then flip and cook 3 minutes on the other side. Set aside while you make the remainder of the Palatschinken.

SERVE: Spread Palatschinken with a marmalade of your choice and roll it as you would tacos.

- Place two Palatschinken on a plate, top with your favorite yogurt, and dust with powdered sugar.

Treasure Boxes

Rakvičky

I think *Rakvičky* (little coffins) is not the best name for a wonderful dessert. They are long hollow pastry shells resembling Chinese fortune cookies in texture but extremely fragile. With the help of my friend, Chef Milos J. Cihelka (born in Prague), the first Certified Master Chef of the United States of America, we changed the English name to Treasure Boxes.

15-20 PIECES
(depends on form)

1 egg

5 egg yolks

2 cups plus 1 tablespoon (300 grams) powdered sugar

1 pkg Dr. Oetker vanilla sugar—or place a vanilla bean into a jar with regular sugar, seal and let sit for few weeks to infuse

3½ tablespoons (50 grams) unsalted butter, for greasing forms

1 cup (250 milliliters) heavy cream, for Chantilly cream

Approximately 20 forms for boxes. If you can't find the same boxes I have you can use any small tart molds.

- Preheat oven to 350° F (175° C).
- Lightly grease all your forms with butter using your fingers. Don't saturate the forms with grease.
- In the bowl of a stand mixer fitted with a wire whip attachment, mix together eggs and powdered sugar on high speed, about 8 minutes.
- When the mixture is fluffy and creamy, add vanilla sugar and mix for another couple of minutes.
- Fill a piping bag with a small nozzle with the batter, and fill the forms only halfway.
- Bake in the oven set at 350° F (175° C) for 10 minutes and see how they rise.
- Then lower the temperature to 200° F (95° C) and bake for additional 15–20 minutes.
- Remove the boxes from the forms as soon as possible after baking, while they are hot.

SERVE: Decorate the treasure boxes as you wish. Use Chantilly cream, fresh fruit, and nuts.

TIP *If the boxes are cold, they will not come out of the forms.*

Czech Pancakes

Lívanečky

The word *Lívanečky* derives from the Czech verb *lít,* which means "pour," as it is a dessert made from poured batter. The word has also spread to Austrian and Bavarian German as *Liwanzen,* or more commonly, *Bohemische Liwanzen.*

24 PANCAKES

2¼ cups (300 grams) all-purpose flour, sifted

⅓ cup (67 grams) sugar

2 tablespoons (20 grams) baking powder

Pinch of Diamond Crystal Kosher salt

2 eggs

1½ cups (350 milliliters) milk

2 tablespoons (28 grams) vegetable oil

¾ cup (200 grams) oil for frying

- In the bowl of a stand mixer fitted with a wire whip attachment, blend the first 7 ingredients until the batter is a uniform consistency.
- In a nonstick frying pan, heat up the oil and keep it on low heat. Make small pancakes using a soup spoon.
- Fill spoon generously with batter and pour it into the oil. Don't try to make circles. Simply stay in the center above the place where you started, and the batter will make circles all by itself. When the spoon is empty, dip the bottom into the frying oil and gently even up the pancakes.
- Fry on both sides until golden brown.
- You may need to add additional oil often.
- Lay pancakes on paper towel to absorb access oil.

CZECH PANCAKES can be served as either a sweet or savory dish.

SERVE with cinnamon and sugar or yogurt and fresh fruit or marmalade for a dessert.

SERVE with caviar, chopped onions, or eggs for a savory appetizer.

Poppy Seed Rolls

Makové Buchty

A Czech classic that brings a whimsical fairytale to life. A Czech boy, Honza lives only for his mother's freshly baked *buchty*. He is a lazy and inept son. One day his mother sends him out into the world to get experience. On his journey, he meets impossible obstacles (most of the time dragons), but he outsmarts them all and returns home with fame and a princess as his wife. When he comes back home, a basket full of poppy seed rolls is awaiting him. Bake these and the entire house will fill with a delicious smell and bring the family together.

18 PIECES

1⅓ cups (300 milliliters) milk, warm

1 teaspoon (4 grams) sugar

3 teaspoons (9 grams) active dry yeast

3½ cups (500 grams) all-purpose flour

½ cup (100 grams) sugar

2 yolks plus 1 whole egg

3½ tablespoons (50 grams) unsalted butter for the dough, melted

1 teaspoon (3 grams) Diamond Crystal Kosher salt (If using another brand, start with half this amount and adjust to taste.)

Butter for greasing the baking pan

Flour for dusting the baking pan

Butter or homemade pork butter for smearing the sides of the rolls

Baking casserole 9 x 13 inches (22.86 cm x 33.02 cm)

SCHMEAR FOR POPPY SEED ROLLS:

1 tablespoon (15 grams) unsalted butter

1 tablespoon (30 milliliters) rum

MELT butter and mix in rum.

- Grease the baking pan with butter and dust with flour. Set aside.
- Stir sugar into warm milk and then add yeast. Let the yeast proof until foamy.
- In the bowl of a stand mixer fitted with a paddle attachment, add flour, risen yeast, sugar, eggs, butter, and salt. Mix it on slow speed for 4 minutes until the dough is smooth. If the dough sticks to the sides of the bowl, scrape it down with a spatula.
- Preheat oven to 350° F (175° C).
- Dust top of dough with flour, cover the bowl with plastic film, and let the dough rise in a warm place until it doubles in size, about 30 minutes.
- On a floured surface, roll dough into a ¾-inch (2 cm) thick rectangle about 9 x 13 in.
- With a 3-inch (7.5 cm) diameter cup or biscuit cutter, cut out 18 circles.
- With your fingers, stretch the dough and place one heaping teaspoon of poppy seed paste in the middle of each circle. Make sure your fingers stay dry.
- Pinch all the sides together toward the center and smear the sides with pork fat, duck fat, or melted butter to make the rolls easy to separate before placing them into a baking pan.
- Smear tops of the rolls with melted butter.
- Bake for 45–55 minutes.
- When still hot, spread the butter/rum schmear on the tops.

SERVE anytime as snack or with coffee for breakfast.

TIP *First cut out all circles, so that if you end up with extra dough you can distribute any leftover dough equally to all 18 rolls.*

Apple Strudel

Jablkový Závin

I wanted to know if my apple strudel recipe could compete with the most famous pastry chefs in the world. In 2003, I purchased an airline ticket to Vienna, Austria, and visited the Hotel Sacher. As I expected, the strudel was wonderful, and it looked exactly like mine. I asked who the master of this strudel was, and the answer was Executive Chef Jaroslav Miller from the Czech Republic. Well, of course I should have guessed it right away. The Czech recipe!

Apple strudel is so good you will want to bake two loaves at a time.

YIELDS 2 LOAVES

Dough for two loaves

2 cups (250 grams) all-purpose flour

⅔ cup (100 grams) Wondra flour or hard red wheat flour

1 cup plus 2 tablespoons (250 grams) unsalted butter, soft but not melted

1 egg yolk

2⅓ tablespoons (30 grams) sugar, for each loaf

Pinch Diamond Crystal Kosher salt

2 teaspoons (10 milliliters) vinegar

½ cup (100 grams) water, room temperature

STRUDEL FILLING

10 cups (1,200 grams) Granny Smith apples, peeled and shredded (weight is after peeling and squeezing out the juice)

SPLIT the total amount into two equal parts.

3 tablespoons (30 grams) black raisins, for each loaf

4 tablespoons (30 grams) roasted pecan pieces, for each loaf

1 tablespoon (8 grams) cinnamon, for each loaf

2 tablespoons plus 1 teaspoon (30 grams) butter, melted, for each loaf

2⅓ tablespoons (30 grams) sugar, for each loaf

EGG WASH FOR BOTH STRUDELS:

3 egg yolks beaten with 2 tablespoons (30 milliliters) milk

- Preheat the oven to 350° F (175° C).
- In the bowl of a stand mixer fitted with a paddle attachment, work all ingredients to create a smooth dough. Divide in half.
- Shape the dough into two balls, cover, and let rest in the refrigerator for 30 minutes.
- Squeeze the juice from the shredded apples. (Drink the juice for health!) Set aside.
- On a floured parchment paper or a clean kitchen towel, roll the dough into a rectangle as wide as your baking sheet.
- On this dough, evenly sprinkle breadcrumbs and shredded and squeezed apples.
- Sprinkle evenly with raisins, roasted pecans, cinnamon, sugar, and melted butter.
- Grasp the edge of parchment paper or towel closest to you and lift it to start rolling up the dough. Let the towel or parchment drop, and continue rolling the strudel, pressing it gently so that it is firm.

- Fold the ends of the strudel under and brush the top with egg wash.
- Slide both strudels onto a baking sheet lined with parchment paper and bake for 35–45 minutes.

SERVE dusted with powder sugar.

TIP *Vanilla ice cream is the best companion.*

Cream Puff Wreaths

Žloutkové Věnečky

Cream Puff Wreaths are among the most traditional and popular confectionery in Czechia. I have to admit that this is my favorite dessert! This traditional Czech pastry is similar to the Italian profiterole.

12 PIECES

PASTRY

1 cup (250 milliliters) cold water

½ teaspoon (1.5 grams) Diamond Crystal Kosher salt

½ cup (115 grams) butter

1⅔ cups (200 grams) all-purpose flour

4 large eggs

FILLING

1¾ cups (400 milliliters) milk

5 tablespoons (40 grams) all-purpose flour

1 teaspoon (4 grams) vanilla extract

3 egg yolks

¾ cup plus 2 tablespoons (200 grams) butter, room temperature

¾ cup (150 grams) sugar

1 cup (250 milliliters) heavy cream

ICING

1⅓ cups (160 grams) powder sugar, sifted

2 tablespoons (30 milliliters) milk, heated

2 tablespoons (30 milliliters) lemon juice

2 tablespoons (30 milliliters) white vinegar

10 grams vegetable oil

Additional powdered sugar for dusting

- Preheat oven to 400° F (200° C).
- To make the pastry, combine water, Kosher salt, and butter in a small pot; bring to a boil.
- When mixture starts to boil, add flour, stirring with a wooden spoon until a white residue forms on the sides of the pot. Transfer to the bowl of a stand mixer fitted with a dough hook and mix slowly until it slightly cools.
- Gradually add eggs one at a time, mixing on medium speed until the batter is smooth, lump free, and soft.
- Transfer batter to a pastry bag with a large-size tip. On a baking sheet lined with parchment paper, form rings about 4 inches (10 cm) in diameter.
- Place in the oven 400°F (200°C), and in 5 minutes reduce the temperature to 180°C (350° F). Bake for total of 20 minutes. *Do not open the oven door during baking.*
- When the pastries are cooled, slice in half horizontally with a serrated knife.
- To make the filling, combine milk, flour, and egg yolks in a saucepan and bring to a simmer. Cook until the mixture thickens, about 6–8 minutes. Remove from heat, cover with plastic wrap, and let cool.
- In the bowl of a stand mixer fitted with a wire whip attachment, cream butter, vanilla, and sugar. Blend in the cooled milk mixture.
- In a separate bowl, whip heavy cream until it forms peaks; fold into the milk and butter mixture.
- Transfer mixture to a pastry bag with medium-size tip; pipe this filling on the bottom half of each cream puff.
- To make the icing, combine powdered sugar, warm milk, lemon juice, vinegar, oil, and whisk for 10 minutes, or until mixture is thick.
- Dip or brush the top half of each cream puff in the icing and place on the filled bottom half. Dust with powdered sugar.